When Mother Cried

An Autobiography

by

Brian Othuke Kokoruwe

North Staffordshire Press

Newcastle-under-Lyme

Staffordshire

When Mother Cried

An Autobiography by Brian Othuke Kokoruwe

All Rights Reserved

© *Copyright Brian Othuke Kokoruwe*

No part of this book may be reproduced in any form by photocopying or any electronic or mechanical means, including information storage and retrieval systems, without permission in writing from both the copyright owner and the publisher of this book.

ISBN 978-1-9160152-3-4

Published in 2019
North Staffordshire Press
10 Queen Street
Newcastle-under-Lyme ST5 1ED

Acknowledgements

The journey towards this book has not been a smooth one, and not something one achieves overnight. First and foremost, my thanks go to my parents. Daddy and Mummy, despite all the challenges faced, you placed me at the top of your priorities within your plans. You gave me the opportunities to develop local cultural knowledge, experience city life, attend the best education and built in me the will to succeed in all that I aim for. You developed in me the determination to work hard towards whatever goals I set myself, and also for me to show compassion and love to everyone of any race, religion, gender, disability or other difference.

There is the risk that I might leave someone out in my acknowledgements. Writing this book has not been easy, not least because of the challenges faced in thinking back to those key moments of my life, and in dealing with the emotions that reflecting on the past brought. At times, continuing with the writing has been very difficult, which meant I relied heavily on others to encourage and support me as this book progressed from start to finish.

In no particular order, I am grateful to the following. I remember, with thanks, the late Mr and Mrs Lowndes – a lovely couple who made me so welcome in their home when I moved to Stoke-on-Trent – who planted the original idea of writing this book. Stephen Bostock gave huge support, in all aspects of the process, and encouragement with collating the ideas and plans; without him, the idea would not have taken off in the first place. My friend, Sarah de Costobadie, a passionate advocate for the English language, gave her wholehearted support, always there to answer questions, along with giving genuine and honest feedback whenever she was called upon. Pete Kalu, a real role model for all the books he has published and for sharing his writing skills with me. To my older brother, Eugene Kokoruwe, who remained patient with me during my 'moments' and was always willing to answer any question I wanted answered. Then there's the Wonderful and Blessed family. Although I did not drag everyone into this work, you were all in my mind and provided spiritual and emotional support.

Sincere thanks to Malcolm Henson and his team at Henson Editorial Services & North Staffordshire Press for showing huge interest in publishing this book and sharing my story. So many other people, such as my friends and work colleagues, have been instrumental in helping me to achieve my dream in one way or another and I would like to say many thanks to all of you.

For Mum and Dad

***

Sweet Mother by Nico Mbarga

Sweet mother, I no go forget you

For dey suffer way you suffer for me yeah

Sweet mother, I no go forget you

For dey suffer way you suffer for me yeah

When I dey cry, my mother go carry me

She go say my pikin, wetin you dey cry yeah

Stop stop, stop stop, stop stop

Make you no cry again ooh

When I wan' sleep, my mother go pet me

She go lie me well-well for bed

She cover me cloth, say make you sleep

Sleep sleep, my pikin ooh

When I get hungry, my mother go run up and down She dey find me something when I go chop

ooh Sweet mother, sweet mother ooh

Son of a sweet mother

When I get sick, my mother go cry cry cry

She go say instead wey I go die make she die

She go beg God, God help me, God help me, my pikin ooh

If I no sleep, my mother no go sleep

If I no chop, my mother no go chop

She not get tire aah

Sweet mother, I no go forget da suffer way you suffer for me yeah yeah Sweet mother

Sweet mother ooh…

"Sweet Mother" Words and Music by Nico Mbarga

© Reproduced by permission of EIT Music Ltd/ EMI Music Publishing, London W1F 9LD

Preface

When Mother Cried is an account of a young Nigerian boy, Brian O Kokoruwe. At the age of three months, his parents had no choice - due to their limited financial situation in the United Kingdom - but to put him on a plane from London to Lagos, to fly under the watchful eyes of the cabin crew. Arriving in Nigeria, Brian's uncle along with his aunty and older brother, Eugene, picked him up from the airport and took care of him for a while in Lagos before Brian was taken to a remote Nigeria village, where he was faced with the challenges and horrors of a Nigerian Civil War. He was later cared for by his grandfather and his grandfather's wife, whom he called Papa and Mama, as he believed they were his parents. As he started to grow up and feel settled with his Papa and Mama, and began to master the local languages, Brian was told that his real Papa and Mama were coming to see him in the village. Confused and shocked, Brian refused to acknowledge his parents when he saw them for the first time. This broke his mother's heart and made her cry.

Brian subsequently lived with his parents then was sent away to school, contracting meningitis, aged twelve. Although he survived the illness, which almost took his life, the delay in treating him meant that he was left profoundly deaf and unable to walk. Without adequate medical resources in the country, Brian's father had to make the decision to send him back to London where he had been born. This was another critical point for Brian and his mother. Losing out on another opportunity to bring up her son, Brian's mother cried as she waved goodbye; he was taken away from her again, this time back to the country where she had given him up.

At the time of writing this, Nigerian politicians are entering a new phase and increased debate about the plight of war. Many Nigerians are anxious for the truth and the consequences of civil war to take centre-stage in these discussions, in order to avoid the risk of history repeating itself.

Malcolm Henson (North Staffordshire Press)

Foreword

When Mother Cried is such an interesting book, it brings out a lot of emotions to the readers. As a friend, am proud of Brian's achievements not just in writing this fascinating book but the determination he shows in everything he does.

Shezad Nawab MBE
Award-Winning Entrepreneur, Interim Executive Director, International Speaker and Management Consultant

Contents

Acknowledgements	i
Sweet Mother by Nico Mbarga	iv
Preface	vi
Foreword by Shezad Nawab MBE	viii
Chapter One: Airmail Baby	1
Chapter Two: Surviving The War	10
Chapter Three: Village Gossip	27
Chapter Four: In Unfamiliar Territory	44
Chapter Five: The Comfort Zone	48
Chapter Six: Sad Goodbyes	66
Chapter Seven: My Move to The City	70
Chapter Eight: Eddy the Monkey	75
Chapter Nine: Murder in The City	90
Chapter Ten: Killings by The School	95
Chapter Eleven: The Deadly Storm	99
Chapter Twelve: What Lies Ahead	130
Endnotes	141

Chapter One

Airmail Baby

It was a bright sunny day when my Mum left Nigeria to travel to join her husband, my Dad, in the UK. In the late 1950s, it was every African man's dream to continue his education abroad, which would give him better employment and lifestyle opportunities on returning to Nigeria. My Dad's dream was no exception, so when, in 1962, he had been awarded a scholarship, to progress his education on an Electrical and Electronic Engineering degree in the UK, he didn't think twice and excitedly grabbed the opportunity with both hands. Travelling abroad for a lengthy period of time wasn't a straight-forward activity, particularly when it involved travelling by air and with a limited luggage allowance. For these reasons, Dad initially decided to travel alone to the UK, leaving his wife, my mum, behind in Nigeria, in order to pursue his once in a lifetime chance. After nearly two years of studying, sorting out a place to call 'home' and acclimatising to the UK weather, Dad felt confident enough to invite Mum to stay with him. Before their trip to the UK, my parents had a son, my elder brother Eugene; they had to leave him in Nigeria, to be brought up and looked after by his grandparents.

On arrival in the UK, Mum was very surprised; not just by the extremely cold weather and tiny houses, but by the unwelcoming attitudes of the local residents. This was something that Dad hadn't warned her about. Men felt it was normal not to be greeted by strangers but women saw this differently. Mum remembered how it was normal in Nigeria for strangers to greet each other. Sometimes they would even join group gatherings, make contributions and be fed, whatever was being served. But in the UK, everyone that Mum walked past seemed to be ignoring her, or simply focused too much on their own business. Mum said she would say, "Hi, good morning," but this fell on deaf ears! Mum felt ignored and so she developed the attitude of not greeting strangers and avoiding those she didn't know. Dad already did that as he had lived in the UK longer than Mum. He didn't want to create any scenes or fuss and so he suggested to Mum that it was best that they kept themselves to themselves. During those early years, they only mixed with those that they knew, either within the local community or in educational or religious environments.

After settling down in London's East End for a short time, Mum received the good news that she was expecting a baby. Whilst this news was exciting, Dad knew it would create some challenges for both of them. Dad was in full time education, with limited financial support, and so he struggled to make a living. In small, shared, rented accommodation, he received a low income from part-time employment and a small amount of financial support from relatives. Mum and Dad faced further challenges. They were unable to secure their own accommodation and, even if they had, they would not have been able to manage bringing up a child, without the support of their parents. Babysitting arrangements would be a big issue. Mum and Dad both needed to work, in order to establish a decent household income. With these thoughts, the happiness of pregnancy and the joys associated with it became worries, anxiety, depression and sadness. Mum, in particular, began to have more sleepless nights and her hormones played havoc with her.

"In the first few months of my pregnancy, I had so many concerns," Mum recalled, "I was so excited about having a little one, who would keep me company when I was alone. I thought that it would be great if we bought a new house but we didn't have the money to do so. We thought about renting our own bigger place, with a separate room for the new baby but in those days it was so difficult for black people to have their own accommodation. I worried about all of us staying in one room with limited airflow. The kitchen was next to the bedroom, which worried me more."

In 1960s England, racism was prominent. Most corners had signage here and there, 'No Irish, no Blacks, no Jews, no dogs'. Opportunities for blacks were limited. Being a black, pregnant woman in those days created extra stress, as getting support through a Pregnancy Support Group or Family Planning Group was very difficult. These struggles led to Dad sending a telegram to his parents in Nigeria, with the good news that they would become grandparents for a second time and he wondered how they could play a part in the upbringing of this forthcoming child. The grandparents were excited and wrote back immediately to their son, suggesting that they could send the child to them in Nigeria, so that Dad and Mum would have fewer burdens and could focus more on Dad's education and building up financial stability for their welfare. Dad received this letter and read it in private. When Mum woke up, he said to her, "I have received a letter from home and they have some suggestions."

Mum was puzzled and, feeling tired, asked him, "What suggestions? To move to a different town?"

Dad silently looked at the ceiling, then through the windows. With a trembling quiet voice, Dad whispered to Mum, "We will send the baby home to be looked after by our parents."

"WHAT?" screamed Mum. "No, no way. I want to keep my baby. I want to spend all the time looking after my baby. Oh no, no." With tears dripping down Dad's cheeks, Mum knew that he had the best ideas for all.

"Listen darling. Life is hard here. We don't have enough money. Our accommodation is very tight. We can't get a job here while I'm still in full time education and it isn't always safe for black children. Our parents will give this child the best upbringing, better than we could ever offer. Please, please, please accept this will be best for the child." Clinching her dress tightly, Mum went silent, looking away from Dad; breathing heavily and trembling, a major flow of tears ran down Mum's cheeks.

"It is best for this child darling. Please listen. Come here, come." Mum did not move. Dad went over to her to give her a cuddle.

This was when Mother cried.

Already missing the son she left behind when she travelled to London, Mum didn't expect to have to send her second child back home to her family to be looked after. It broke my mother's heart that she would have to let go of the baby that she had carried for over 38 weeks. During those weeks of her pregnancy, Mum recalled her moments of emotional roller coaster rides and those moments when she was excited and had both day and night-time dreams of how her London baby would be treated in a very special way. This baby would have the best doctors, nurses and a safer environment, from birth through infancy and into adulthood, despite the hassled surroundings they faced on a daily basis. Amongst Mum's Nigerian friends in the UK, she would be the first to give birth here. Mum would be the one who would act as a model mother, an expert in all areas relating to not just motherhood, but for mothers in a foreign land. Deep down though, Mum was worried. How will the baby be registered? Will he or she be registered as a British Citizen or a Nigerian one?

Or will dual nationality be possible? Many of these concerns Mum left to Dad to research and deal with. For Mum, her sole focus was to make sure that the baby would be healthy, well fed and safe.

In those days, for many people, the main way to communicate was through face-to-face communication. You either visited those you wanted to talk to, or they visited you. This created moments of isolation. One was stuck with one's own gossiping neighbours or, alternatively, rather than face-to-face, one could send a letter, which took days. If you had a car, you drove around often, to catch up with family and friends. For those who had no car, they walked, took the bus or used their bicycle. "We didn't use taxis much in those days," recalled my Mum. "Money was difficult to earn. We rarely used them; we either walked or took the bus. I stayed in most of the time rather than go out in the cold. I only went out when it was absolutely necessary. If it wasn't urgent and I could stay in, I would. Your dad did most of the shopping, visiting and planning."

Traditionally, Nigerian men had greater authority and flexibility with movement. They made most of the important and vital decisions affecting the family or their partner and went wherever they wanted to go. They were the head of the house, similar to Nigeria being governed by the Head of State or the military ruler. Men decided what to eat, where to go, when to return home, what to do and what not to do.

Nigerian men had authoritative powers. Women generally respected the men's decisions on religious grounds; the man was believed to have been created first, followed by the woman; they were seen to have greater knowledge and experience with everyday living. These traditional views were obeyed by Nigerian women in that era. Women rarely challenged the decisions made by the men, whether they liked it or not. While these cultural beliefs were established in Nigeria, they were also respected and followed by Nigerians outside their country. While they were in the UK, they brought along with them Nigerian traditional beliefs: women were to respect men, children to respect their parents and all elders. They were seen to be wiser than younger people and therefore elders were not to be challenged. In the absence of parents, the eldest member of the family took on the decision making. In most cases, decisions made by the men were not to be questioned… whether women liked them or not. It was not uncommon even for men to decide what clothes and shoes women should wear. A man chose the television channel to watch! He had sole access to the bank account and he was allowed to withdraw money at any time. Women weren't allowed to withdraw money without prior permission from the man. Men could go out without telling the woman where they were going or when they were expected back home, but a woman could not do so. While a woman would carry the unborn baby for months, after the birth the man was responsible for most decisions pertaining to the life and bringing up of the child. He decided on the child's name, which school it was to go to and the child's further career paths. A woman stood back and appreciated whatever the man had decided. It was not a surprise when the decision that the man had made went wrong; the man sometimes blamed the woman for not assisting him to look at the other side of the coin! This was sometimes the cause of rows in families. The man, cheekily blaming the woman for decisions that he has made, without the woman interfering, was unjust. Life in those days wasn't fair.

My mother cried. It was too much to let go of her newborn at only three months old. Mum continued to cry until there were no more teardrops. Her dear baby son gone far, far away, leaving her with only three months of memories to cherish; they held Mum together during good days, but on bad days, the thoughts of not being able to see, hold and share her tiny baby became too hard to bear, so strong was her affection as a mother. My mother cried again and again, despite being a strong daughter, a strong lady and a strong mother; being apart from her little baby aroused emotions within herself that were too hard to deal with.

It was when I asked about my grandparents, that I learnt some interesting facts. I had many grandparents. My mother's parents were my grandparents. My father's parents were my grandparents. There were many other older relatives that I knew to be my grandparents but there were two sets of grandparents that were really close to my heart. One set was so close, I saw them not as grandparents but as my parents. They were the 'parents' that took care of me from a few months old. Grandfather Chief Kokoruwe Agboge was a farmer; he was married to Grandmother Avwioroko Olokor. However, as Grandmother Avwioroko Olokor was unable to have a child herself, she arranged for her husband, Grandfather Kokoruwe Agboge, to marry a younger woman to bear him children. For this reason, Grandfather Kokoruwe Agboge accepted a second wife, Grandmother Eyadorobor Titi Okumakugbe. The three of them lived happily in Iseulugu, where Grandmother Eyadorobor Titi Okumakugbe later gave birth to Wilson Diejeta Kokoruwe, who subsequently married Julie Comfort Ossom. They had their first child, Eugene Kokoruwe, while they lived in Nigeria. My parents moved to London, where I was then born. Life situations following my birth forced my parents to send me to Nigeria, when I was three months old. There were struggles to decide about which set of grandparents would care for me: initially, my mother's parents, the Ossoms, took care of me but my father's parents, the Agboges wanted to. Finally, my Dad's parents gained custody and took responsibility for my welfare, however, as my mother's parents also lived nearby, my time with both sets of grandparents was shared. It was the Biafran Civil War that split our families and which forced others to relocate across geographical and tribal boundaries.

Chapter Two

Surviving The War

Anyway, we all had dreams, my friends and I. In that way, all children across the world are the same. In Nigeria, the best prospect in life for most would be to join the army but that was something I could not have done. I didn't want to have to shoot and kill other humans at the bidding of another man. I could have been a doctor and tried to cure those who had been hurt by soldiers. There were not many Nigerian sports heroes to look up to; although the Nigerian national goalkeepers received some attention, this was nothing compared to the publicity given to English and Brazilian strikers that we heard about on radios daily. There were no televisions in most houses. If we wanted to watch anything, we went to the nearest house with a television and peeped through the outside windows, as not everyone was allowed to go into the living room of other's houses, particularly children from other families. Most of the time, we simply waited for news to come to us from whoever had heard the news from the cities. The villages rarely had electricity, let alone a television, but some houses had their own generators and did have black and white televisions. Cassius Clay was known all over the world, and Nigeria was no exception. I loved him because he was a one-man hero.

The earliest memories I have are from when I was about three years old, a child in the Nigerian village of Iselegwu. Even then, I understood the importance of working to survive. My grandmothers didn't have the choice like some in England, to stay at home and look after the children. Everyone had to work. Grandma and her friends would walk miles to the market to sell dried fish by the basket load. Every morning, young and old men would wake up to go fishing, and would supply my grandmother and other women with fish to sell. Fishing was the main source of income for most of the villagers; without it we would not have been able to survive. Grandpa contributed extensively to the household income by cultivating various products from his farms. What he was able to cultivate for both grandmothers to sell, depended on the season. There was the corn season, yam season, pepper season, okra season, cassava season, bitter-leaf season and so many other little vegetable seasons. In addition to these vegetables, sometimes Grandpa successfully hunted some wild animals that he brought home for dinner, for my grandmothers to sell or simply to share with our neighbours.

My grandmothers often asked me to go to the market with them. I would always refuse because I didn't have the patience to stand in the heat for hours, waiting to sell all of the fish. Sometimes I would go fishing or to the farm with my grandfather, but I was never allowed more than a yard or so into the river. People had been attacked by snakes and other animals in the past. My grandfather taught me so much about life and there are lessons of his that I will carry with me for as long as I live.

When I was growing up in the village, I always felt different to the other boys. I knew which hospitals or homes my mates were born in, as they would regularly point to their birth place; strangely, neither I nor my friends knew where I was born, as I couldn't point to anywhere. I'd try to ask my grandparents, but they couldn't state a particular location. I wondered why. Was I not born locally? Was I born in a different city far, far away? My grandparents would not answer. I wondered why they hid that from me. My thoughts wandered away to a different country. I didn't know if there was a different planet from earth in those days, I knew there were other cities, states and countries but that was all. Unlike the other children, I had clothes and didn't wait for anything like school books, school uniforms and so on. My grandparents bought them for me, as soon as they were requested by the school. Some children did not even have enough clothes with which to cover their bodies. I was always well fed, whilst the other children could not be guaranteed three meals a day. My grandmothers brought different friends and relatives to meet me. Everyone wanted to hold me and seemed to admire me. I was too young to understand why and I soon grew tired of people coming to greet me or to check how I was doing. Some brought sweets or fruits, which I didn't want to eat. Food items weren't of interest to me. I would rather go out to play from morning until bedtime with my mates. We would go out to climb trees, jump down from as high as possible, or simply play various games. That kept me from over-eating - I was a very over-active child.

The mystery of where I was born continued to float around my head at every given moment, until one day when I heard my Grandma Eyadorobor Titi telling her friend that I was from London, and that was where my parents still lived. I didn't know what she meant. I had never heard of London. I didn't know that my grandparents weren't my real parents, even though they were much older than the other children's.

Not long after my third birthday, the village was invaded without warning. There were no telephones for people to contact us to warn of any impending dangers; even though we had radios, the news was not very up-to-date either. I didn't understand what was happening as a group of local village men ran over to our home and spoke urgently with my Grandma Avwioroko. Everyone was panicking. My Grandma Titi, who was also listening nearby, quickly ran outside to the neighbour's front patio where I was playing and picked me up, dragging me by my right wrist, then leading me inside the house. I could only stand still with shock, wondering what was happening, as both grandmothers began to throw whatever items were close to hand, into bags. Grandpa Kokoruwe soon dashed over, rapidly picking up whatever he could get his hands on, squeezing them into empty bags he found and getting us to run through the back door, which was nearest to the woodlands.

We all headed for the bushes; despite being filled with dangerous animals, foliage would help to prevent us from being seen and caught. Even though my grandfather had a shotgun, cutlass and other hunting tools, we were still not entirely safe. It was very late and dark by the time we could stop rushing through the bushes, and we could barely see in front of us. Granddad's shotgun and other hunting tools wouldn't be sufficient to protect us from what we couldn't see. When we stopped, I couldn't sleep; it was hot and dark and I just wanted to go home, eat and rest. I was scratched, battered and bruised by the forest thorns but I wasn't allowed to scream. My whole body itched, but I couldn't scratch - scratching itchy skin would only make things worse. There were various native leaves that were rubbed on my skin to stop the itching. I really wanted to scream but I always had to be quiet, so that nobody could find our hiding place. Grandpa would lead us - sometimes he wasn't sure where we were going. We would rush northwards, then rush back southwards, westwards then eastwards. We had no map. I felt really disgruntled, as I was so tired and hungry. With us being lost in the middle of nowhere, I felt even more fed-up, irritated and discontented with the whole drama - I loved playing in the bushes, they gave me the opportunity to misbehave, kick trees, throw sticks around and bite and chew some edible fruits. I felt a little at home while I was playing temporarily in the bushes, but after days without a break, I began to hate them and everything that was in them. I just wanted to go home, take a bath, eat and sleep. I wondered when we were going home; we never used to rush to go to the farm. We didn't need to carry so many items for farming and I wasn't usually rushed out from the house to go there. Grandpa didn't bother if I stayed at home and then either Grandma or both of them would bring me to the farm later. With all four of us rushing rapidly, I could tell we had no idea which farm we were going to and for what reason.

I didn't know it at the time, but there was a civil war being fought. The war that had started further up in the north of Nigeria some months earlier, had finally reached us in the south-eastern part. There was a division between the North and the South, in the wake of Nigeria's independence. There were varying religions and cultures in Nigeria and they had spread out across the country; when the conflict began, people were subjected to extreme violence, or even murdered because of these differences. It didn't matter if one was a male, female or even a child. Those obsessed with getting control of power or just keen to kill others from a different ethnic background or religion, just wanted those that stood in their pathway gone. There were many lifeless bodies scattered around. The sadness of the war! It is said that between one and six million Nigerians lost their lives to fellow Nigerians, all for the sake of gaining control over the Biafra region; to prevent Biafrans from gaining independence and to keep Nigeria a unified country.

Living in the forest during this time of war was extremely difficult for all of us. I wasn't used to being uncomfortable and without luxuries, and we constantly had to be on the move to avoid being captured. Likewise, Grandpa fought and struggled through the wild forests, fetching whatever he could to feed us. We lived on roasted yams, plantains, fruits, coconuts and local river water. It was a journey that I felt was going on for ever and ever.

I remember hearing several gunshots; it was so scary. I wondered if they would get to us. Grandpa would tell us to keep quiet and encouraged us to keep moving; being an experienced hunter, he knew what to do, when to do it and how it should be done.

On our escape journey away from home, I saw that the ground was splattered with the blood of people who had been badly injured, but we couldn't stop to help them as it was still a very dangerous time and we had to keep moving. There were also mutilated bodies and corpses lying around; I was too young to associate the mutilated bodies with the war, but as I grew accustomed to the violence, I realised that those people had lost their lives and I felt we were so fortunate to have ours.

After travelling, for what seemed like a lifetime, we heard the sound of people celebrating in a forest village. As we came nearer to the crowd, I could see that Grandpa and both grandmothers recognised some of the people from our previous village.

Finally, we knew that we would be safe.

When we eventually came up to it, they spoke different languages but Grandpa spoke them too! Both grandmothers worked together and supported each other's needs however they could. They were like sisters and, for me, I was glad that I had two 'mothers'. When one was tired, the other took over enabling one to take a rest or focus on other things such as cooking, fetching water, picking fruits. One stayed with me and perhaps Grandpa would go hunting for something for our meal.

In the new village, they appeared very friendly and welcoming. Grandpa found a spot to settle down in, and built a mud hut, with a thatched roof made of dried straw and palm branches. We had been sleeping rough with some local village people who gladly welcomed us. Until Grandpa built our home, the four of us shared a tiny space wherever we were offered one to sleep in for the night. We were glad to have a new place we called home. This new house that Grandpa built in Iluelogbo was very elegant, even though it had no toilet, bathroom, running water or electricity. Most homes were like that and some didn't even have doors inside the house, just cloths to cover the entrance to each room, which had no windows. Outside there was the door into the property and a few little window spaces, again covered with cloths - like curtains but with no locks. On the outskirts of the village there was a communal toilet, and we got our water from a well, which was near our home. Our main source of light was from lamps, powered by kerosene or candles. The streets weren't lit in the evening however we became used to walking in the darkness, which was brightened by moonlight.

The long journey had come to an end. Grandma Avwioroko, being much older than Grandma Titi, wanted to do more for the family. She spent a lot of time looking after all three of us. Not long after the war, Grandma Avwioroko went regularly to the farm to cultivate various items like cassava, peppers, okras and other vegetables. On one such occasion, when we were all at the farm, Grandma Avwioroko stepped on a sharp object amongst the debris; she let out a loud scream and fell to the ground. We rushed to her, Grandpa fetched some local leaves, squeezed them together and dripped the liquids onto the wound. This was the villagers' treatment for cuts. However, the cut was so deep, it appeared to have sliced her foot nerves and veins. Grandma Titi tore a piece of cloth from her wrapper, which she used to tie up the wounded leg to limit the bleeding but still the bleeding continued. We took her home, called local native doctors and also those who had some medical knowledge. It was a few days later that it became clear that the wound had become infected and there was nothing else that could be done to cure the injury. Without local anaesthetic, they relied on Grandma Avwioroko's bravery to amputate part of that leg, just below the knee cap. Hearing Grandma Avwioroko scream was so upsetting. I cried. I felt her pain and shock and the sadness of losing part of a leg and the disability that would go with it. She would miss farming, carrying heavy loads on her head from the farm, dashing here and there getting things together for family meal times. There was so much that Grandma Avwioroko would not be able to do. She continued to scream in pain - louder and louder. I wasn't allowed to watch but hearing her scream was enough aural information to tell me that she was in awful pain. After a moment, she went quiet. I thought there had been a magic cure for the injury and Grandma Avwioroko was now pain-free and would be able to return to normal life. I saw her briefly and held her hand a bit, she stroked my hair, pulled me to her and gave me a cuddle. Then I was told to go to the other room and I went there. Lots of elderly people went in to see Grandma Avwioroko and suddenly there were screams and cries. I was shocked again and didn't know what was happening. Later on, I was told that she had passed away. I cried with the others around me, even though I didn't understand what passing away meant. I imagined that she would come back from her sleep and be with us again; just as we were before the war.

Grandma Avwioroko survived the perils and tragedies of the civil war, but for her to be killed by a lack of medical attention still upsets me. The Biafran War, as it became known, lasted from the 6th July 1967 until the 15th January 1970.

Life after the war was very quiet as so many of our friends and relatives had lost their lives in the fighting and now we were in a new village, with different cultures and different languages. They spoke Urhobo or Isoko, while in our previous village the languages were Kwale or Ibo. There were so many funerals taking place each day; funerals became a way of life. Many people had died, and their family members, if any were left, went to the bushes to seek the bodies of their loved ones, to take them to a convenient resting place; others died slowly while back home as a result of wartime injuries or even due to malnutrition. Everyone in the village knew many people who had been killed and life was never the same again. I helped to tidy up the village alongside other children, under the supervision of elderly people, who directed us. There was debris everywhere to clear up and many homes didn't look like homes any more. Some were completely or partially burnt, others had visible bullet holes in the walls; sometimes I found used and damaged bullets, plus several live rounds of ammunition. We worked hard for months to build a new home and to get back to a normal life. No matter how busy we kept ourselves, no one was able to forget the nightmare that we had lived through.

Although I was distraught at the loss of my Grandma Avwioroko, there were some children who had lost their entire family. I couldn't imagine how painful that must have been; we helped by taking in some of those who had been made orphans by the war. They became my friends and, soon, more like siblings; we were happy together, but in the back of our minds, there were always painful memories of the war and of people who had been lost.

For several years we tried to return to our previous home but had to wait until it was officially safe to do so. Grandpa did eventually return there and reported back to us. He told us how he had found several blood stains on the walls and the roof was blown off.

The war forced us to flee from Iselegwu to Iluelogbo; we still kept our home in Iselegwu, as Grandpa had farms there along with some of our friends. So, to this very day, our 'homes' are split between the two villages even though we live in just the Iluelogbo one.

When I was almost six years old, the opportunity to start school came. Grandpa enrolled me in the local primary school. I had lots of new school uniform, general casual wear items made especially for me and several new pairs of shoes were bought for me too, for the start of the academic year. The clothes were made to measure and the shoes came from outside our village because the village shops did not sell many high-quality items. In fact, most villagers didn't wear shoes and their clothing items were very basic. Boys and older men were usually content to have on shorts and whatever vest they could find. There was no wardrobe full of clothes. Most people had only about three items, so each was worn frequently. The good thing was that the extreme high temperature meant clothes could be washed in the morning and within an hour or so, they would be dried and ready to wear again. Village clothing items didn't include socks, so most people didn't have any.

Villagers who needed footwear wore basic handmade sandals, some crafted from local tree trunks or whatever materials they could find to create them. In those days, everyone was content to have just anything to wear as clothes. Most little children wore nothing more than shorts.

Smartly dressed with white socks and shiny black shoes, I rode to school with Grandpa on a bicycle, sitting on the back, square metal seat, behind the rider's triangular seat. Even though I had been treated to a new school uniform, I didn't want to leave Grandpa to go to school. After he had dropped me off, I would run back, chasing him and hoping he would take me back to the farm where he was going or allow me to stay with Grandma Titi to do whatever she wanted to do that day, however Grandpa would turn back, riding towards the school. I would stop, stare at him and wait for him to leave. Grandpa would drop the bicycle, take me by my hand and walk me into the classroom, making sure that the teachers kept me with them.

When I did go to school, the other children gave me weird looks, which was probably because of my smart uniform and new shoes. A lot of the children couldn't afford to have school uniforms made or bought for them, never mind the shoes; most went to school barefoot and had only their shorts on with a vest. The teachers were always kind and understanding; they knew that many children were orphans of the war or their parents didn't have much money as most of their belongings had been destroyed, so children weren't punished for not having a complete uniform. All the teachers cared about was that the children learned something every day; in order to help with this, we were given homework and tests very regularly. Lessons were taught in the native Isoko language and not in English. Most people at that time, even the teachers, did not understand English.

Whenever we had tests or exams, if a pupil scored below the pass mark there was always a punishment. Normally it would consist of being called to the front of the class, kneeling down and raising your arms above your head; the worse the performance in the tests, the longer you were left to kneel down. Some of the children, who had lived in other villages, spoke different languages, which made it very challenging to be educated in Isoko language; probably their previous language might have been Urhobo, Ibo, Kwale or some other language.

Iluelogbo Primary School was built in a corner of the village; unlike most buildings, which were built with red clay, the school was made out of cement. There were gaps where windows and doors should be, but nothing was installed. There was nothing in the classrooms that could be stolen or damaged. Each one had only a blackboard and the teachers took the white chalks with them at the end of the lessons. The furniture was extremely sparse; the children sat on the floor and the teacher had one desk, which she or he also used as a chair. The most popular subjects were maths and biology; they were useful for teaching us how to manoeuvre in the market place, or to understand about living creatures and illnesses.

Life in our village meant that few children fully applied themselves to getting an education. It wasn't their fault. Most families wanted their children's help on the farm or in the house. They didn't understand what education was for. There weren't many jobs, which required qualifications, only teaching really, and there were few positions for that. Being able to progress with education past school age was a privilege that was reserved for the rich, and many pupils left school and went straight to work on the farm. These families didn't see the point of wasting valuable support opportunities on the farm by their children sitting in the classroom instead.

Unlike my old village before the war, the new settlement village was very different; there were no large rivers, which had a near endless supply of fish, so the villagers there didn't place such a high value on fishing skills. Instead, Grandpa had to cultivate his plot of land; this took a lot of work on his part as it hadn't been worked on since before the war.

Early every morning, Grandpa used to ride his bicycle to the farm - the journey could take up to two hours each way. I was still too young to be of much help on the farm, but I helped in any way that I could and picked up many useful skills from watching Grandpa. We used cutlasses for the weeds, and collected dried branches of trees for firewood. We would create huge heaps of weeds and tiny branches from trees, which we would set on fire. This process had to be repeated several times because the farm had been left to grow unrestricted. Soon there was enough space to plant important food products like yams and cassava, even peppers and vegetables like corn and okra. This was how I spent my weekends in the village and I always looked forward to spending time with him.

When I turned seven, Grandpa told me that my parents and siblings would be returning from London to live in Nigeria. I found this incredibly daunting at first; I had been brought up by my grandparents and had no memories of my parents or siblings. I didn't even know what they looked like. Since the war, life was starting to become normal again, I had my friends, Grandma and Grandpa, and I didn't want any more changes. Most of the village people believed that my grandparents were my Mum and Dad; there were only a few relatives, who knew the facts. I couldn't understand why my parents wanted to come back, but they wanted to return to where they were born, to their parents and friends, and their sons.

Chapter Three

Village Gossip

It didn't take long for word to spread across the village that I had other parents and that my grandparents were not really my Mum and Dad. Many people asked me questions about them but I had no answers to give. I asked my Grandma and Grandpa a lot of questions after my parents had decided they were going to come back; Grandpa managed to find some old photographs so that I could see what they looked like before they travelled abroad. I expected them to look different but had no ideas what they would look like. When I saw the old photos, I refused to believe they were my real parents.

The couple in the photos would go on to have a child named Brian Othuke Kokoruwe. I wasn't always called Brian though; it wasn't a popular name in Nigeria and many people in the village struggled to pronounce it. When I was little, I was called various names and I answered to all of them. Most people called me by my native local name 'Othuke', which means 'God's strength', but my parents had told my grandparents to ask people to call me by my English name. Sometimes I was called Ibraham, Abraham or Braham and because I didn't choose my own name, I didn't have the right to refuse the other names, which people might call me. The villagers were more familiar with these names because they had heard them in the Bible during Sunday service or Bible studies.

Grandma Titi was a very religious woman and she attended church as often as she could, sometimes going four times a week. Her priority was always to devote what time she could to God. She was an especially kind woman and I admired her greatly for this. She always showed kindness to others; in fact I think she was incapable of hating anyone. Grandma Titi particularly disliked violence and devoted much of her time to helping some of the more disadvantaged people in the village. She would offer food or drink to anyone who came to her. Sometimes, as a child, I fought with other children who wanted too much of our food. Grandma Titi would tell me off and allow them to eat and drink until they were fully satisfied or until there was nothing left, just like family members.

I tried to emulate a lot of Grandma Titi's principles; I grew to love God and attended church regularly from a very early age. It wasn't always an easy path to follow; sometimes, I would be tempted to miss church, when given the choice between staying with friends and playing football, but my faith remained strong. I have always believed that even though people sin, God would always love and care for them.

My grandfather wasn't a religious man, but he never tried to discourage anyone from believing. He would always welcome my grandmother's Christian friends to the house and make them feel comfortable. Sometimes they would talk to Grandpa about the importance of attending church; he would listen politely and carefully but as he was often tired from working, he would tend to fall asleep if the conversation went on for too long or go into his room and nap. If I was seated next to Grandpa during house Bible studies, I would try to shake him discreetly so that he would wake up. I would often laugh about it, but he always said that he wasn't asleep, just listening very carefully.

Like my Grandma Titi, Grandpa was a kind person and didn't approve of violence. He was always happy to keep himself to himself and wasn't the kind of person to interfere in other people's business. The only time I ever saw my grandparents argue was if they both wanted to take me somewhere at the same time. Usually they came to an amicable arrangement and one would agree to take me with them the next time.

I will always remember what Easter Sunday Eve used to be like in the village. Grandma used to get us ready at 9pm. Once dressed, we would light a candle and join all of the other Christians. We would all march like armies, holding up our candles or lamps, and head to a large point in the forest, just at the corner of the village. People joined as the group marched past their homes. There were approximately 150 in the group, of all ages. Everyone used to sing loudly and this would wake more people up, who would come to join us. Even though the village was not that big, everyone felt like one big and unified family. Villagers who weren't Christians knew about the annual event; they didn't mind, because we all accepted each other's differences. By the time the procession had arrived at the park there were volunteers there. They would arrive early so that they could prepare meals for the attendees to eat. The meal was paid for by the church and of course the money came from the congregation; it consisted of fried rice called 'Jollof' rice, with assorted fried fish, chicken and/or beef as side dishes.

For weeks after Easter, the party was all that we would talk about. Many of us, especially the children, wished that it could happen every day even though it was a very tiring day for us. Staying awake through the night and marching all day with nowhere to sit was extremely difficult and then after we had reached the park, we would play games for the rest of the night, laughing, eating and drinking Coke, Fanta or water. When the event had been completed, which was around 2am on Easter Sunday, everyone would then gradually go to their respective homes. We would all get ready again and attend church at 8am on Easter Sunday; not much sleep but still we were all so excited and happy! Easter only came once in a year and it was to celebrate the life of the Risen Christ.

Eventually, a day was confirmed for the arrival of my parents. They would be bringing my brothers and sisters with them - I had mixed feelings about this. Although I was excited at the prospect of having an extended family, which would be arriving from abroad, I was nervous. They were a complete family, who had always known each other - in the way that I had my grandparents and friends in the village - so what if I didn't fit in with them? They would probably speak English or other languages, which I may not understand.

In the days leading up to their arrival, I couldn't help thinking about how my life would change. I liked my simple village life but this wouldn't be something that my parents and siblings would be used to. The more I thought about their upcoming arrival, the more withdrawn I became from my village life.

My family arrived in the southern part of Nigeria; once the news reached us, the preparations began immediately for their arrival. The party for my Dad's homecoming would be unlike anything which had taken place in the village before; he had left the country years ago, and hadn't returned. The entire village was proud of him for going to England, gaining university degrees and achieving his career goals.

The food began to arrive first: a large cow was delivered, as well as several live chickens; live goats, yams and rice. Then came the extra pots, oil and large batches of firewood that were gathered from the forest; all would be needed for cooking such a large amount of food to feed a whole village. The villagers all helped to erect tents, and chairs were brought from the church and town hall, so that people could sit comfortably. There were decorations everywhere. I had never seen anything like this, and all for the family that I would be reunited with. As I helped my grandparents and the other villagers prepare, I forgot my fears and worries. I was now proud of the family that I would be meeting and I was at the centre of the excitement surrounding them.

I didn't enjoy observing the animals being slaughtered but these were being done in public view and anyone could watch. It was normal. Lots of children, both boys and girls gathered around the poor animals being slaughtered. I think that they were more interested in what delicious meals they would be cooked into, but for me, I felt sorry for these poor animals and chickens. It took over two days to cook and prepare everything. Crates of beer and soft drinks were arriving daily and Grandpa arranged to have a new suit made for me for the occasion. The night before their arrival I hardly slept; Grandpa and Grandma had a lot of friends over, who were helping with the final preparations, so it was impossible to get much sleep. Most of the helpers also slept in our house.

My family arrived at the village in a convoy of new cars. Back then there weren't many cars in the village at all; we mainly used bicycles or walked. Villagers had lined the streets so that they could get a glimpse of my family as they came into the village for the first time. The convoy of cars had their horns blaring loudly on arrival at the village entrance. There were drummers and dancers showing the cars the route they should follow to the party destination. The crowds of people were making me feel nervous. I would be meeting my family for the first time, but with the whole village watching me. Guns were fired into the air when my family got out of the car and many of the villagers were cheering loudly in their excitement. Even the children, who were too young to understand, were screaming so that they could join in the dancing.

I started sweating and just wanted the noise to be over. I knew my grandparents were excited; after years of only communicating with their son by letters and telegrams, now they would see not just their son after so long, but also their grandchildren. When my family got out of the car, I could hardly see them; everyone ran out in front of me to greet them, and I was too small at the time to see over them.

They were led immediately to the chairs which had been brought out from the school and reserved for them. I assume that one of them must have asked for me because quickly all heads turned to look at me and people began to usher me towards them. My grandma came through the crowd and led me by the hand to my parents. There was a man sitting down, who had a beard, and he held his hand out to me. I didn't know how to respond. I was told that he was my father but I couldn't look him in the eye. I was scared of the man with a beard as not many men in the village had beards - all men shaved daily. I hadn't seen men with beards except those who were homeless and insane in the streets. They were scary people, as they slept rough and sometimes had no clothes on; people detested them.

My mother didn't really look like me or the villagers. Her complexion was much fairer than ours; it hadn't occurred to me that the sun makes us darker and it made me feel as though this new family was already very different from me. My parents must have sensed that I was worried because they held on to me very tightly. I noticed for the first time that there were two boys and a girl, standing nervously behind my parents, who were staring at me. The boys were wearing suits that were much smarter than mine and the girl had on the loveliest floral dress that I had ever seen. They were all speaking a different language which I can only assume was English.

I can't begin to describe how strange it was to be reunited with the family that I couldn't recall and to hear them speaking quickly to each other in a strange language. I didn't know what they thought of me or the village. As soon as my parents loosened their grip, I ran back and vanished into the crowd, refusing to return to them.

Food and drinks were served to my family on the reserved table; I stared over at them cautiously from a corner, while they ate. Even though - to me - it wasn't very hot, they were sweating profusely. They also seemed to be finding the food too spicy; they were drinking a lot of water with every mouthful. The more time I spent watching them, the more I realised that they were poles apart from me.

Once they had finished eating, they watched the dancing and **circuit** shows that the village had organised in honour of their arrival. Native music was played but I doubt that they were able to comprehend what the songs were about because their understanding of the language was non-existent. Despite this, they could not have failed to be impressed with the ceremony itself; the entire village had turned out and there were entertainments to suit everyone.

The adults danced through the night until the sun came up but many of the children dozed off, as the event went on into the late hours. I stayed awake for as long as I could. I wanted to be there for the entire event, but eventually I too fell asleep on the chair and I could not remember how I ended up in my bed.

My grandmother woke me up early the next morning and informed me that my father wanted me to go with them and my siblings to the city of Auchi, which was about 4 hours' drive away. I refused straight away. I had only just met my family and couldn't imagine leaving the village and my grandparents behind, to go with virtual strangers to a part of the country which I had never seen. My grandfather negotiated with my father and they managed to agree on leaving me behind until they were more permanently settled. I will always be so grateful to my grandfather for giving me the extra time with him and my grandmother in the village.

Despite this disagreement, we all ate together before my parents departed. It was difficult, because we couldn't understand each other; I spent most of my time looking at the ground, avoiding eye contact and trying not to communicate at all. Eventually, a friend of my grandmother was able to act as a translator and I began to learn about my family. The older boy was my brother Eugene. He was born in Nigeria and taken to England as a young boy. The younger baby boy, Benjamin, was also my brother and he was born in Cardiff, Wales. The impeccably dressed little girl was my sister, Edore. Although none of us had much time to converse, the translator was kept busy helping my grandfather and parents to communicate. It was still nice to learn their names and to know about where they came from.

My siblings from abroad stared around my grandparents' house; they must never have seen one like it before. I secretly observed them as they tried to avoid touching things; as though touching the items would hurt them or cause them harm. They had grown up experiencing an entirely different world, one that I couldn't really imagine. I wanted to ask them so many questions but even if I could have spoken their language, I'm not sure if I would have been able to ask them any questions as I had no imagination of the world that they had come from or what kind of food they ate there or things that they did there. They might have thought my questions were stupid or pointless so I kept quiet and let my thoughts just wander around. Even then, I was always shy so I struggled with communicating with those I did not know very well.

Each time I looked at the window and saw my friends peeping at my new family and I, I had a big grin on my face. I am sure they would have swapped places with me if they could. I was the centre of attention because I was a member of the new family, that had travelled to Nigeria after being abroad for such a long time.

As soon as they left for the city, my friends all rushed towards me. Anthony was my best friend and he wanted to know if my family had given me sweets and other goodies, how I was feeling and which language they were speaking. Even though the questions sounded easy, I couldn't begin to answer them. It was nice to meet my new family members but I didn't want to go and live in the city with them. Here I had the freedom to go out to play with my friends, whenever I wanted to; and my grandparents would know that I was safe. I was the only one that my grandparents would focus on and they were the only people I looked up to. I imagined that in the city, life would be different. I wouldn't be allowed to go out to play whenever or wherever I wanted. Even then, who would I play with? My mates would be in the village and my family didn't speak the same language that I spoke. I was so anxious about so many things, deep inside me; I was filled with sad emotions and became withdrawn from all around me.

My friends and I mainly played football. The goal boundaries were usually made of several shirts dumped about six steps apart at each end of the field or if there were long sticks, these were hammered into the ground using our bare fists. Sometimes, I didn't know whether or not to laugh when there were arguments about whether the ball had crossed the line or not; if you happened to have the strongest boy in your team, you had a better chance of winning the arguments and possibly the game. There was no referee or linesmen. Any one of the players, particularly the goalkeepers, acted the roles of referee and linesmen.

The main attraction of football was the idea that if you were good enough, the school PE teacher would notice and you could be selected to represent the school against other schools in competitions. The fun thing with this was that team members had the opportunity to travel in a bus to other towns. For many kids, there were no other opportunities to leave the village. Inter-school competitions gave the opportunities to travel across village boundaries and to meet other people outside our village. These were very good educational opportunities too, as we learnt that other village or city people didn't speak the same language that we spoke in our village. They also wore different clothes and their food preferences were very different from ours too. For some, this also led to the opportunity to play for the State team, then possibly for the Nigerian national team. That was the long-term target for most of the boys of my age. The girls weren't really involved in sports; they didn't play football and mostly did needlework and handicrafts. I supposed that the girls wanted to work in the market after school. Their ambitions were limited as, at that time, most ladies in the village focused on looking after the household.

I remember that, when I was little and living in the village, my State had won the Nigerian main inter-state championship trophy. At the news of this success, all the villagers danced in the streets and celebrated wildly. Footballers were celebrated heroes of the country and so they were idolised by many. This in turn, made the football players rich beyond their imagination; their successes brought them both government and private-sector funding. They all lived in the biggest houses, drove the nicest cars, they had the best clothes and the most beautiful girlfriends. The older I grew, the more I realised that the footballers' lifestyle didn't appeal to me, as I began to learn that many people thought of footballers as people who didn't have the determination to succeed in school and I didn't want to be thought of as a lazy and uneducated boy. Grandpa had told me that the pathway to success in life was through education, but how? I didn't know, but then I respected Grandpa and believed all that he told me; after all he always wanted the best for me.

Eventually, news came that my father had written; he wanted me to go and stay with him for a week's holiday in the city. It would be exciting to see other places; I hadn't ever been far from the village before. I told my friends about it and they became quiet. It is possible that they thought I wouldn't come back to the village after the holiday.

A few days before my parents came to collect me, my grandparents took me shopping. They bought me lovely new clothes and a new pair of sandals, to make sure that I wouldn't look out of place when I went to the city. I am sure that they knew that the city people didn't dress like villagers.

By the time my parents arrived, I was already packed and prepared for the long drive to the city. It would take around four to seven hours, or so I was told. My grandparents made sure that I had eaten properly. Along with my father and siblings was my cousin, Isaac, whom I had not met before. They only stayed for about two hours, then we were expected to start the journey to the city. Along with my luggage, my grandparents had packed some of my favourite food in various containers, bagged them and put them in the boot of the car. I was struck by how thoughtful this was; I hadn't thought that there would be nothing to eat for seven hours or so. I didn't even think there would be hunger during the journey. Grandparents knew best! They knew also that I had so many questions about what the city would be like and I had wondered whether the food would be different to ours. My grandparents had also packed our local food items in the car boot, that could be cooked for me in the city, so I would not feel homesick.

My friends were in the street, watching us prepare to depart. I didn't know what to say to them, and my siblings were trying to talk to me, but I still couldn't understand them. My grandparents hugged me and told me to have fun and remember to behave. Just before I got into the car, I ran to my friends and their parents that were nearby. I hugged them for what seemed like ages. Tears rolled down my cheeks as I said goodbye to them. I was called to get into the car. Slowly, I walked towards it. The rear door was opened for me, I got in and sat next to the window so that I could see the villages as we drove through them. Once the car began to drive away, I waved goodbye to my friends, their parents, others in the streets and especially to my grandparents; my father pulled me back so that I would sit down, instead of standing peeping my head through the window. I waved out of the back window, faster and faster as the car pulled away and I carried on waving long after they were out of sight.

I was about eight years old and this was the first time I had ever travelled in a car; we didn't even see cars very often in the village streets, they were mainly only on the high roads and were usually for the shop or business owners. I hadn't been inside one before. It was certainly faster, and more comfortable than a bike! My father and siblings would often look at me and speak but this was the only way that I could assume they were addressing me; my English was still very limited. Even if I could have communicated with them, I wouldn't have wanted to. I was enjoying watching all the villages and forests fly past as we drove along. This was the first time that I had seen so many new places.

I spoke very little during the car journey; I was too preoccupied, thinking about the things that were ahead of me and those that I had left behind. Fortunately my cousin Isaac spoke my language, so at times he was able to act as an interpreter between me and my immediate family. Driving to the city, we encountered and passed by several market traders; they stood at the edge of the roads, selling food to passers-by - something like a one-man service station. Halfway through the journey, we stopped and bought peanuts and roasted corn, which we ate in the car together.

Although being in a car was an exciting new experience for me, the journey wasn't especially smooth for me; every time we drove down a hill, I felt like throwing up. We arrived at a petrol station and the smell made me vomit without warning, but I couldn't explain this properly to my family, due to the language barrier. Luckily, I was able to give clues that I was about to vomit so Dad pulled off the road, stopped and let me throw up. This happened many times, throughout the journey. I could tell that Dad was very frustrated and annoyed about it, as I had interrupted his rapid dash back to the city but, I couldn't help it.

By the time we arrived at my parents' house, most of us had been asleep for several hours. For the others, they were arriving home and they were pleased but I felt nervous in the unfamiliar surroundings. I came out of the car behind everyone else. My mum was there to take my hand and show me into the house. I sat down and was very impressed with it; it was decorated beautifully and there was electricity and also air conditioning. I was very tired, but Mum insisted that I showered. I can only assume my father had told her that I had vomited. There were different kinds of soap and the towels were softer than I had imagined they would be. When I finished, Mum was waiting for me with new pyjamas, which fitted perfectly. After a dinner of rice and stew, I was nearly asleep at the dinner table, at which point I was taken to bed.

Chapter Four

In Unfamiliar Territory

I woke up early the next morning. I was unsure of what to do, so I waited in bed until the others woke up. My mum came into my room, saw that I was awake and brought me a toothbrush to use before breakfast. This was the first time that I had used a proper toothbrush and toothpaste; in the village we used traditional chewing sticks and we simply rinsed our mouths out with salt water, scrubbing our teeth, using our fingers tips or toothpicks. When I went downstairs, I was shown how to switch on and off the electric light and how to use the television, but changing the channels took longer to get used to, as there were too many buttons to press and I worried about damaging it. Even then, there weren't many channels where they spoke my village language so I simply watched the television, amazed by the scenery, the clothes they wore, the language they spoke and many more puzzles. I wondered how the cartoon drawings were able to move and talk, cry and show emotions. When a character died, I felt such pity and emotion; this put me off watching too many programmes. In the villages, we rarely saw or heard of people dying, except through old age, accident or illness. Here on television, there were people of all ages and even cartoon characters dying. I thought these were all evil, real and sad.

I remember before I left the village, my grandparents had told me to behave and I didn't want to let them down by damaging something in my parents' house, as all of their things appeared to be very expensive. I still felt that I was a visitor; I didn't feel that I belonged to the city house. Breakfast was a bowl of cornflakes, which I had never seen before. I was asked if I wanted any more but I shook my head, as Grandpa had taught me that it was impolite to ask for more food in someone else's house. Even though I was technically with my family and could do as I wished, I still didn't feel comfortable doing this, like I would with my grandparents.

Then a second plate of fried eggs, baked beans, fried tomatoes and onions arrived; everyone had the same thing. We all had knives and forks and I wasn't sure what they were for, so I thought it best to wait and see what the others would do. My father began to eat first; he held a knife and fork in each hand and began to use them to cut up and eat his food. He sat opposite me so I copied him. I began to try and eat with the fork in my right hand and the knife in my left so Mum came to me and swapped them over.

Now that I was holding my knife and fork in the correct hands, I had to try to learn how to use them; I had never fed myself with them before. I ended up holding my knife and fork and just staring at the nice smelling meal on my plate. Fortunately, Mum noticed and asked me if I would prefer to eat with my hands. I was just about to grab the egg when she waved to stop me; she wanted me to wash my hands first, so the maid brought me in a bowl of cold water. After washing, I was about to grab the food when Dad shouted at me to use the knife and fork. After that, Mum seemed to have told him to leave me alone and let me eat, so he kept quiet and, without looking at anyone, I ate nervously and as quickly as I could - thoroughly enjoying the meal with my hands.

Once the meal was finished, the maid cleared the table and arranged the washing up. My parents took me to visit some of their friends who lived in other parts of the city. My siblings also came; they all spoke English, which I still didn't have a good understanding of, so I said very little and was very quiet and still. All of their friends always spoke to me and often they would shake my hand or come to sit next to me, even though we couldn't understand each other - but I just wanted to be left alone.

I often felt uncomfortable, despite everyone being nice to me. I wished that I was back with my friends and my grandparents, but there was no turning back now. I had to stay for the rest of the week with this new family. My father's friends advised him that it was important to break down the language barrier before anything else; otherwise we would be like strangers forever, always speaking in broken sentences or through another person or gestures.

Every day I met new people; some we went to visit and some came to visit us. The food was normally very nice; there wasn't much that I didn't like. I particularly enjoyed the sugary food items. In the village, we had little sugar and my food was chilli-based. Here in the city, there was very little chilli in the food items; even my sister didn't seem to eat any chilli at all and I noticed Mum had prepared different chilli-free food items for her. Interestingly too, my brother didn't eat fish, so Mum also had to prepare separate fish-free dishes whenever Dad wanted us to eat fish-based meals. Mum also tried to cook traditional Nigerian food. I think this was so that I would be made to feel more at home.

I didn't have any friends in the city so this meant that I was housebound most of the time. Sometimes I would go out with my brothers and sisters to play ball games in our back garden. We also used to cut empty food tins and other used items, like Coca Cola caps, into smaller shapes and compete to see who could design the best toy car. We were always told by our parents not to play this game because the sharp pieces could cut us and cause an infection, so we would have to work quickly at designing them, to create them before Dad came in from work. Mum wasn't so much of an issue because when she was at home she was often occupied with the cooking, housework or entertaining friends.

Chapter Five

The Comfort Zone

My sister Edore didn't normally play the car building game with us but she would often get involved and acted as judge, by deciding which car was the best once we had all finished building. She liked to talk a lot, and she would often try to make me learn new words. Whenever I learnt one, she would run back to Mum and inform her that I had spoken more English words. This often made me feel embarrassed; my little sister was behaving like a teacher which made me feel like an incompetent pupil. I didn't say much, unless it was necessary, as I couldn't always be sure that I could pronounce words correctly.

My mum also tried to teach me how to say new words. When we were having breakfast, she taught me how to ask for more food. Most of the time, I wouldn't ask for any more, as I didn't want to be greedy but also because I didn't know how to ask for more in their language. When I asked for more bread to go with my breakfast, or at least that's what I thought I had said, everyone started to laugh hysterically and I began to wonder if it was silly of me to ask for some, or thought it might have been rude of me to show a lack of satisfaction with the morning meal. My older brother, Eugene, was the first to point out what I had said. Whilst laughing he informed me that I had asked for 'more breast' not 'more bread'. Perhaps my native accent had contributed to this or my lack of knowledge of the English language. In the village our word for bread was 'loft' so it was a completely different word to me. After that I was reluctant to ask for anything more and always settled for what was on my plate.

The day before the end of my holiday, with my new family, was the longest one. I didn't understand clocks at the time, but I could tell from the strength of the sun roughly what time of day it was. I kept walking out of the bedroom or peeking out of the windows to gauge how long before I could go back to my village home. My experience with my new family was mixed; I had enjoyed getting to know them all better, but I still felt uneasy. I was also becoming extremely bored because there was nowhere outside for me to play, other than in our back garden.

In my mind, I compared the village and the city lifestyles, and I asked myself which one I would prefer to live in. I enjoyed the food, comforts and cleanliness of the city. I also liked the beautiful houses and the bright lights at night time. However, I missed the freedom of the village, my grandparents and my friends. I knew that I would prefer to live in the village; I was happy in my village home, even without electricity and though my grandparents' house was not beautiful, it was still the home which I had grown up and been happy in.

The evening arrived slowly, and I became more excited to think that the next day I would be returning home to my grandparents and my friends. I thought they would all be waiting to see me and that they would have lots of questions about my time in the city. I wondered what had been happening in the village since I had left: what I had missed and what might be new. Even though I had only been gone a week, some of the days had felt like I had gone out of the village and into the city for weeks. Some days were really slow as I was bored and stuck indoors watching television programmes that I didn't understand. I never recalled feeling like this when I was in the village because there was no television; we always had so much to do there and I was rarely indoors except for food or bed times.

On the final day, we ate our breakfast very early. Only a few of us would return to the village but we didn't know who would be joining us. Dad had kept it to himself. Now that my English was getting better, I was able to join in with some of the conversations with my new family at meal times, but not much. I didn't understand everything so I made sure I smiled regularly, so as not to appear rude. I was also smiling because in a few moments, I knew I would be on the journey back to the village to see everyone whom I had been missing - particularly my dear grandparents.

We were still speaking at the table when Dad arrived. He had been to the petrol station and had bought me some clothes, socks and two new pairs of shoes to take back to the village. I was very excited to receive these gifts and my siblings waited for theirs, only to receive one item each. Edore was the first to complain about this, quickly followed by Eugene. My mother could see that they were unhappy, but she supported my father for buying me more gifts to take back; they already had lots of nice clothes, shoes and toys, which I couldn't have imagined previously. Mum appeased them by promising to take them shopping a few days later and with that the conversation returned to normal. I think that Dad had gone to get the petrol without me as he knew that the smell of petrol made me vomit and didn't want me to be sick on the journey back to the village, disrupting his smooth drive.

My time with my parents was starting to run out, so my mum took me upstairs to begin packing. Once this was finished, I went back downstairs to the living room to watch television with everyone. Most of the programmes were in English; it was only part of the regional news programme that was spoken in the native language and that was infrequent. I wasn't overly concerned with the television as we didn't have one in the village and I had been fine without it, whilst my siblings seemed to be quite addicted to it. When I got to the living room there were more friends of my parents who had come to meet me, so again I murmured a hello and smiled. Mum asked me to come and sit by her, while my siblings began to gradually leave the room. I guess they had become bored of the conversation but it was worse for me, who could understand much less of it than they could. I wanted to join them but it would be rude to leave the room when people had come to see me. They didn't stay long and as soon as the visitors' car left, my siblings returned.

Dad announced the plans for the trip back to the village. Only Dad, Mum, cousin Isaac and I would be going on the journey. My siblings weren't happy about this plan as they wanted to go too. I didn't know if this was because they liked it or if they just wanted to come for the long drive. The drive to the village meant that they could see different parts of the country and get away from the routine of the city. I imagine they found the village a dramatic change, just like I found the city to be. They started to pull Dad's clothes, screaming and throwing tantrums as they wanted him to change his plans. Dad finally did and allowed both Edore and Ben to join us on the journey too.

Dad didn't tell them what time we would be leaving, and the afternoon carried on through to the evening, when we settled down for dinner. We all went to bed much earlier because we were going to travel very, very early in the morning and because Dad wanted to drop me and return back to the city the same day. I was playing football with my friends in the village in my dream when I was suddenly woken up by my mum. The lights in my room weren't switched on, which was disorientating. She told me that we would have to begin the long journey soon, as it was safer. The road conditions weren't totally favourable; tyres would burst, bumpers and exhausts would often fall off cars, due to large potholes and, because they were costly to repair, they would simply be left by the roadside where they fell off. These often damaged other cars, when they were driven into during the darkness or on flooded roads. Most drivers had some mechanical knowledge and would patch up their own cars whenever it was possible, unlike in England where MOTs are a legal obligation. I often felt sorry for those on foot, motorcyclists and bicycle owners because the cars would often bully them off the roads, and accidents or even death weren't uncommon.

The boiler had been on through the night, so there was plenty of hot water for showers, unlike in the village where we didn't have hot water. We usually bathed in cold water or if we wanted warmer water, we would boil a kettle or pot of water, which we poured into a bucket of cold water - this was generally done outdoors. After my shower, Mum had placed my new clothes on my bed so I could wear them on the journey back.

Once dressed, I went downstairs; I could smell cooking and when I arrived at the dining table I could see my father was absorbed in some paperwork. We ate and drank quickly because I could tell that Dad was in a rush to start the journey. We always knew Dad was in a mood when he was very quiet! Dad's quietness usually told more stories than when he spoke.

Mum called Isaac to bring my luggage down from my bedroom, while we hurried out to the car. It was still very dark, like midnight, but I think it would have been around 5am. Dad and Isaac sat in the front and Mum sat in the back with me. I wondered how my siblings would feel when they found out that we had gone without them! I was unsure when I would see them again and, thinking that they were coming with us or at least that Edore was coming too, I hadn't even said goodbye to them. My thoughts quickly turned to my grandparents and if they would be home when we arrived in the village, but I hadn't thought that it would be bright daylight by the time we got there.

I must have fallen asleep because I was startled by a bump and when I opened my eyes the sun shone into them immediately. I wasn't sure where we were or exactly how long we had been travelling. When my father noticed that I was awake, he told me that we were near a village called Onitsha, which was a couple of hours away from our home village. I was disappointed that we were still so far away, but I was excited that I was closer to home. A moment later, as we began to drive downhill, I started to feel ill. Mum told Dad to pull over quickly and in no time I threw up. Dad didn't look impressed and Mum was glad that I hadn't thrown up in the car, as that would have made Dad even more furious. My tummy calmed down and I remained quiet for a moment. I fell asleep again for nearly an hour and was woken up by my mum, asking me if I wanted anything to eat. I had groundnuts and roasted corn, the same things I had on my journey to the city.

Soon I began to recognise the surroundings; I knew the village and my grandparents weren't far away now. I wondered what questions my friends would ask me about my week away and if anything would have changed? When we arrived, my grandparents rushed outside before I had even had a chance to get out of the car, and I knew they must have missed me a great deal. I was surprised to see a lot of my friends with them; while I had been away, they had made sure my grandparents had their company and helped them with their work whenever they could. I was so grateful to them for this, but everyone in our village was like a huge family, and we all helped each other whenever it was possible.

My grandparents and I rushed over to each other. My parents remained at a bit of a distance; perhaps they thought that I hadn't enjoyed my week with them after all. I could smell food cooking when we all got into the living room; a traditional dry fish eugsi soup and pounded yam were the favourite meals of the villagers and within fifteen minutes we were eating. I wanted to go and see my friends, and I could tell they wanted to hear about my experiences, but before I had the chance to run off Grandpa told my friends that they should come back in an hour or so. While we were eating, I answered all of my grandparents' questions about my week in the city in the native language. I told them that I had enjoyed myself. My parents saw my positive facial expressions; even though they didn't fully understand the native language, this seemed to please them.

Once I had finished eating, I asked Grandpa if I could go outside while he spent time with Dad and Mum. Grandpa gave the go ahead and said I mustn't be far away. I ran outside to my friends before my family could be told where I was going and why.

My friends who were nearby quickly fired one question after another at me regarding my trip; many of them were trying to speak over each other at the same time. I quietened them all down and told them about the long journey, the television, the new clothes I had bought and my boredom at not being allowed to play outside whenever I wanted. I was impressed by how clean and bright the city was and the lovely English food which my Mum had cooked. I explained to Grandma about all the new food that I had in the city which I had never eaten before in the village. Food items such as spaghetti Bolognese, pasta, cornflakes, omelettes, chips and porridge, I also mentioned about how bread was sliced, toasted and buttered. Grandma was really puzzled. I could tell she had no ideas what those foods tasted like or what they looked like, but her positive nods told me that these were all kinds of food that she wouldn't mind trying. I was about to continue explaining my experience in the city when I heard Grandpa shouting my name. I was told to come back to the house to say goodbye to my parents, before they returned to the city. I still felt awkward approaching them; I hadn't known them for very long and wasn't sure what to say. My mum hugged me and told me to be good and Dad pulled out several notes from his wallet and handed them to me. I didn't know what I would do with all this money; I had never had so much before. They left very quickly after that. Perhaps they wanted to get the long journey out of the way as quickly as they could before it was dark.

Grandma Titi offered to take care of the money for me. I was too young to go to the shops alone to buy clothes or toys in the village and I only ever needed a few coins at a time to buy sweets. I was excited to show my grandparents the presents that I had been given: my pyjamas, clothes and shoes.

Grandpa Chief Kokoruwe Agboge was a gentleman. Here he is with his first two wives: Grandma Avwioroko (left) and Grandma Titi (right), and also my older brother Eugene.

Myself, brothers Ufuoma, Eugene, Benjamin, Obuko and uncle Samuel. Sadly my youngest brother, Obuko (second from right) who was the youngest in the family, passed away due to diabetic complications. He had inadequate treatment and lacked diabetic management knowledge.

At Hillyfields, Ladywell Park, Lewisham, South East London. This is at the park, where I learnt to regain my balance and I 'started' my athletics career from here. Dad got me my first car – a Beetle. I had no driving licence then but rather than leaving it idle in London, Dad transported it to Nigeria for family use. I had heard rumours that adult relatives and my uncle had suggested that it wasn't safe for a deaf person to drive a car. I was encouraged to work hard to gain good qualifications, which would help me to achieve jobs that would come with a personal chauffeur, so I wouldn't need to learn to drive!

Dad, Chief Engineer Wilson Diejeta Kokoruwe he was always smartly dressed and studied at Universities in London, Salford and Cardiff. Dad also worked at the BBC, before returning home to be Head of the Electrical and Electronic Engineering Department at a major petroleum training organisation.

Family photoshoot: brothers Eugene, Benjamin and Ufuoma with sisters, Edore, Ovo and baby Ono. I was not yet with the family.

At my school fancy dress party, I had the chance to dress up as a soldier. I felt good, but the thoughts of the war put me off chasing a career in the army.

I loved boxing. I was very impressed with the skills of Muhammad Ali. "Float like a butterfly, sting like a bee."

Mum dressed in her Indian outfit. She had many friends from different cultures and always tried to match their cultural-wear when they went out.

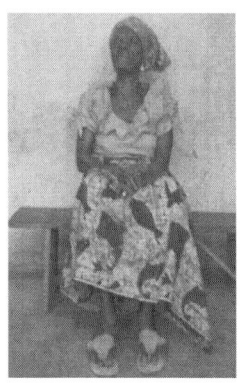

Grandma Titi. She was Grandpa's second wife, being introduced to Grandpa by his first wife. He then married Grandma Titi and she became his second wife. Following the death of my first Grandma Eyadorobor just after the war, Grandma Titi brought me up.

A good get-together with my brothers and sisters in the village. We all now live in different parts of the world!

Dad (white trousers) with his friends and relatives.

Mum (second from right) with my uncle, auntie and relatives whom I lived with temporarily when I returned to London after catching meningitis.

At my 7th birthday party, I wasn't fully 'ready' for such 'big' celebrations. I was used to just sitting down with my grandparents and a few friends during my birthdays. We ate simple food like jollof rice and fried chicken and drank water.

Left: At Government College, Ughelli, Delta State, Nigeria. A photo session was arranged for my friend Ugo and myself with our House Trophies. The bully guy in the middle wouldn't let us take a photo without him and forced himself between us!!

Visiting the village is always fun: a full family get-together.

Mum dressed up for church. She has always been a dedicated and committed Christian.

With Dad during his 80th birthday party, in Isoko village. It was a special occasion and most of the villagers participated in one way or another.

Me with brothers, brother-in-law, Mum and Dad, at Dad's 80th birthday party.

Sisters get together at Sister Ono's wedding to Dion.

Behind me is the house where I grew up, just before the Biafran war.

Me in front of the outdoor bathroom.

The Iselegwu river is still a major source of livelihood for the locals, who depend on fish and water from the river.

Chapter Six

Sad Goodbyes

A few months later after the end of the second term in Primary 3, my Dad came back from the city to visit. This time he brought along my sister, brothers and Mum. He left us at home then, went to my school with Grandpa. There was no room for them all to stay for the weekend so they had to go back to the city immediately after Dad and Grandpa returned. This meant Grandpa was left to tell me about what had happened. Grandpa explained that Dad was keen for me to learn English. I wondered why. Then he said that Dad was considering transferring me to a more advanced school in the city. I was stunned; I didn't want to leave my grandparents, to learn English or to live in the city for any reason.

Grandpa's voice was emotionless. He must have discussed it at length with my father because he sounded completely accepting of the decision. I knew that, given the choice, Grandpa would have had me staying with him and Grandma Titi forever. I had been living with them since I was a baby and now I was finally coming to the age where I would be able to help them as they grew older. Knowing that if I left them in the village, I couldn't have the opportunity to do that, upset me a great deal. I knew my grandfather very well and he always considered his options very carefully before coming to a decision. He was one of the most sensible men that I knew and very well respected by the villagers; knowing this made me feel slightly more reassured by his decisions. He informed me of the plans and felt that they were for the best. Even though I knew that, it upset me to know that I could no longer help Grandpa on the farm, I wouldn't be able to fetch fire wood and water for my grandmothers, or keep them both company.

When I returned to school the next day, my English teacher asked me to wait for him after the end of the lesson. He told me that my father had spoken with him and that he was keen for me to improve my English as quickly as possible. My father wanted me to be able to hold a proper conversation with him and my siblings; the time when I would live with them was fast approaching and it would be very difficult to carry on in the way we had, when I had stayed with them previously. I was also told that he wanted me to go to university eventually, and that English would be essential for working through my education and for any job, which I may wish to progress to.

I had never given any thought to university, much less the idea that I would have to learn a new language to help me fit in with a new family. My teacher and father were in agreement that there was no future for me there in the village and that I wouldn't be allowed to end up an old man working on a farm. But that would have been more than enough for me; I had been happy with the idea that one day I would take over from my grandpa on the farm. I was already very familiar with how things were done. Now, the language that I had spoken my whole life was something which I was told was meaningless and not useful outside the village, and I was expected to follow in the footsteps of a man, who I still didn't really know, even though he was my dad.

I still didn't know what my father had done in England or what work he was doing now that he was back in Nigeria. Despite all this, the decision had been made for me. It had also been decided that I would have to undertake extra English lessons, to prepare me for my new life, as the few hours English lessons a week in school weren't enough to help me progress at the rate which would be necessary. It was so strange to think that one day I may be going to England, like my father had, and studying at a university there.

The closest I ever came to thinking about England, was when we saw flying objects in the sky. The science teacher told us that they were called aeroplanes; they took people to different countries over the sea; far-away places like other African countries, Europe and America. For a while I thought that these places were in the clouds, as I had never seen a plane on the ground, and that there were people who lived above us in them too. Sometimes I would stare up at the sky with my friends, trying to see the people who lived there, but we were never fortunate enough to see them. We even tried to see those inside the flying objects, but could only see faded images on rare occasions.

Chapter Seven

My Move to The City

As time went by, I saw less of my friends, we visited each other a lot less and I didn't have as much time now that I was taking extra English lessons. I think it was difficult for them to understand what was going on; I had really mixed feelings about moving, while they were sometimes jealous of the opportunities that I would have. I also wanted to spend as much time as I could with my grandparents, now that I would be leaving to live elsewhere. They really appreciated this and we managed to get a great deal of work done on the house and farm in that time.

I was also really happy to learn that my grandparents wouldn't be alone once I had moved out. I had a cousin called Afigo, who lived in the next village, and it was arranged for her to come and live with them so that they would have help as they got older. She moved in before I left and, although she was very quiet at first, she became like an older sister to me as time went by. She was even able to speak Basic English, which was considered a very impressive ability by many of the villagers and it was useful for me to have someone to speak English with apart from my teacher. Afigo was always happy to help my grandparents, often completing tasks before she had been asked, and I really liked her for that. I felt happier knowing that, though I would not be living with them for much longer, my grandparents would be well looked after by someone who also totally cared for them.

One day we received a letter from my father, which informed us of his plans to come and collect me from my village, once he, my mother and siblings had moved to Warri, a city around an hour and a half drive from the Iluelogbo village where I lived. By the time they had fully relocated to Warri, there had been a new arrival; I had another sister, named Ovo. When Dad came to fetch me, he brought her with him - my grandparents were so excited to see her for the first time. She was their fifth grandchild, and the second girl. Saying goodbye to everyone wasn't as difficult as it had been the first time; I knew that I was moving to a place which was much closer and that I would be able to visit if I wanted to.

When we arrived in Warri, I saw that it was much nicer than Auchi. It was considerably smaller, which made it feel more like a village, and there were woodlands which surrounded it. The language, which was spoken here, was also much more similar to my own and it made me feel much more comfortable, as my English still wasn't perfect. I began to settle in and was enrolled at Igbudu Primary School; it was only fifteen minutes walk from the house and on the way to my dad's place of work, so Dad's driver was able to drive my siblings and I to school before taking Dad to work.

Igbudu Primary School was near the river and next to the army training base. The school was built with white blocks, which were smoothly plastered and painted a cream colour, there were concrete floors and the roof was made of zinc. Unlike my previous school, Igbudu Primary School had wooden windows and doors which the school locked after school hours. The classroom had minimal furniture, but more than I was used to seeing and using back in the village. There were small desks and chairs in the classrooms, but not quite enough for the number of pupils, so the earlier you arrived the more likely you were to have somewhere to sit. There were normally around thirty pupils in a class and we would have one teacher, who was responsible for teaching us all of the subjects. Some pupils had to share a chair and desk if they arrived late.

There were some distractions at the school; every now and again we could see the soldiers performing their marching drills. Sometimes during break periods, my friends, some other pupils and I would stand near the fence and try to imitate the soldiers and the army commander, although I'm not sure if the soldiers were pleased about that. We realised how hard their work was from the suffering etched on their faces - strict drills had to be perfected in extreme heat and wearing thick combat clothes, boots and hard hats. There was also a market nearby and it had a lot more variety than the one back in the village. Sometimes my friends and I would go over to look at all the toys or simply to buy ice cream, which they sold there; I would completely lose track of time and sometimes arrived too late for lessons. I didn't have a wristwatch and it wasn't easy to tell the time. Usually the school bell informed us of when it was break, time to return to lessons or the end of the school day. This wasn't something which the teachers were concerned with on a daily basis, as they were only too eager to punish us for being late, either using thick ropes as whips, rulers or by simply making us kneel down with our hands up in front of the class. Also, all pupils had to take exams and by missing lessons, they would be missing vital information that may help them pass the exams.

Despite sometimes missing lessons, I usually achieved average grades in the exams, although I really hated science and geography and I was still struggling to make sense of some of the English words; I therefore found myself underperforming in those subjects. Dad wasn't happy when he looked at my results and saw that I had achieved some low grades; he suddenly became very strict on all of us. He imposed constraints on the hours we could stay out to play; gave us timetables covering all the subjects we did at school and for when we had to do our homework. When my siblings and I returned from school, we would have to stay in and study until late in the evening. Once we had finished, we ate our dinner, stayed awake for a bit and then went to bed. It wasn't fun staying in to study after a whole day at school, but Dad rewarded our good performance, so that encouraged us to put in a bit more effort. The rewards were usually simply congratulations, rather than goodies like sweets and ice creams. For performing well in our exams we sometimes got extra clothes, shoes or more pocket money.

Chapter Eight

Eddy the Monkey

During the weekends we had more free time, and one such weekend we went to visit my auntie and uncle who lived in a particularly far away village. When we arrived, I was excited to see that my relatives had caught a monkey; it was a grey African monkey and one of the cutest creatures I had ever seen alive. It was extremely restless and always moving around to see what was happening nearby. The monkey was being kept in a cage so my siblings and I pleaded for it to be let out.

Our cousin got a lengthy lead and collar to put around the monkey, so that it could be let out without causing any damage; it was for the best that he did this because the monkey jumped at us, as soon as it had been let out of the cage. I could see that my mum was very scared; she tucked her legs underneath herself so that it wouldn't be able to reach her. I was the first one from my family to approach the monkey. I had seen many similar ones in the village, but had never been close enough to touch a living one before. I stretched out my right hand, which was clenched with nothing inside it; the monkey was immediately interested and playfully tried to see what I was hiding. We started to play and muck around and became close to it - it would be a good pet, I thought.

The monkey was really friendly, but also extremely mischievous. We took it around the house, playing and giving it the freedom to do what it wanted, but with a lead and under our supervision. It was always trying to grab various objects and throwing them at us or wherever it wanted. We would try to educate and discourage it from doing so. If it damaged things, it had to be placed back in the cage, which it didn't like, and so it learnt not to do things that would make us put it back in. We noticed that the monkey was also fond of grabbing fruit from wherever it saw some, whether on the table or if people had fruit with them, and then it ran away even though it was on a long chain. My siblings and I spent the entire trip playing with the monkey and we begged my auntie and uncle to let us have it. Somehow, we persuaded my parents to agree to let us keep it and we spent the whole journey back home excitedly chattering about what to call it, where it would sleep and who would feed it.

Even my mum softened towards it and was much less scared, now that she had become used to it. My dad wasn't too eager about the monkey; he probably saw it as another thing which would stretch his financial resources, but he saw we were very happy with it and imagined that the new pet would keep us indoors, which in turn would encourage us to study harder.

When we arrived home, we put a small collar and chain on the monkey to stop it from running into the road. The home it had come from was much smaller than Warri and the monkey wasn't used to so many cars. No matter how many bananas we fed it, it would always still want to grab whatever anyone around was eating, but this never bothered us as we saw it as funny. We all used to love watching it climbing on ropes and trees; it was fascinating to see that it never fell off or injured itself like we would have. After much debate, we eventually decided on a name and called it Eddy.

Eddy felt much more like part of the family with a proper name, rather than us just calling him 'the monkey'. Once, somebody accidentally left the door open to the dining room after the house maid had left breakfast prepared for my dad. Dad came in and saw Eddy sitting in his chair, halfway through his toast, having already finished his milk for his coffee. From then on, we had to make sure that everything on the table was covered, even if it was only going to be there for a moment. Eddy brought a lot of fun to the family and we all bonded a great deal because of him. Instead of going to the markets after school, we would hurry back as quickly as possible so that we could all play with Eddy.

I hadn't made a lot of friends at the Igbudu Primary School, but I did make friends with the next-door neighbours' children, and their parents were friends with mine. They used to come over to see Eddy too; he was very popular in the neighbourhood. When Eddy had become more accustomed to his environment, we let him off his lead and allowed him to roam freely around the garden. We had a twelve-foot fence around our house, and many trees; although he was perfectly capable of climbing over the fence, he never left us.

Sometimes he would climb to the top of the highest tree and not come down until we tempted him with bananas. Quite often, he would take one from us and climb back up the tree before we were able to get him, and he repeated this process four or five times, until he had all of the bananas in the house in his possession. I think Eddy thought that all the bananas in the world belonged to him, because he would always try to grab them from anyone who tried to eat them in front of him; if we wanted to eat a banana, we had to make sure that Eddy wasn't in sight.

Edore would often go to visit the neighbours, on her own or with me, and Eddy would accompany her. The neighbours had a large German shepherd dog that wasn't very friendly. Eddy used to take advantage of the dog's short temper and would throw things at it from a distance. The dog would get furious and attempt to attack Eddy, but Eddy was always too fast for the dog and would climb up the trees, teasing the dog from there until the owner came to restrain it and Eddy came down and jumped to us. It was real fun having Eddy with us for such long while.

Sadly, we woke up one morning to find that Eddy was struggling to move. We knew that this was unusual because he was usually always up before anyone else in the house. We were all still very young at the time, I was only about ten years old, so didn't fully understand that Eddy wasn't able to tell us what was wrong with him. He died before we could even get him medical attention and the whole family was very distraught. We did ask Dad if we could have another monkey but he didn't think it would be fair on the monkey or on us. We were all heartbroken for a long while and felt great sorrow for the loss of our dear pet.

To cheer us up, Dad took us to see my grandparents in the village; I had been missing them a lot, and my siblings enjoyed the change of scenery from the busier cities which they were used to. I would go and stay with my grandparents some weekends and during the holidays, and I always loved going back to see everyone, including my friends. I would bump into some of my old school teachers too. The English teacher would speak English with me. He was impressed that I spoke English back. He would then speak the native language, Isoko, to make sure I still understood it. I would respond to him in whichever language he chose to communicate with me in. He would tell me how he was always telling my former classmates that I was now speaking good English and that if I could learn it, so could they.

We were hit with more bad news, not long after Eddy had passed away; my grandfather had fallen ill. I rushed to the village with my parents, so that I could be with him and my Grandma Titi. My father made sure that Grandpa was taken to the best hospital in the region and he was given the best available treatment immediately. Sadly, he was not fully better when he was discharged even though the doctors had done all that they could for him. We were all glad that Grandpa could come home, but worried about whether or not his health would hold up in the future.

My father suggested that, instead of bringing Grandpa back to the village, he would be better looked after if he lived with us in the city. It would mean that my dad could look after him and that when he was at work, there would always be someone in the house who could make sure Grandpa was okay. It would also mean that if Grandpa fell ill again there would be better means of transporting him to a nearby hospital. The village didn't have many telephones and nobody had a car because there was no need to travel very far. Many of the villagers had only seen passing cars but never ridden in one. When anyone was poorly in the village, it was the case that the doctor or a medical know-how person would be called to visit the sick person in their home. They usually rode there on bicycles.

We all felt much better when Grandpa agreed to come home with us to Warri. We hadn't expected him to agree without an argument because he was such a proud, independent man who valued his independence. He even seemed excited at the prospect of spending time with his child and grandchildren and also with eating some of the food which was not so readily available in the village; things like cornflakes, baked beans and pasta. He also liked to drink Ribena and other fruit juices, which my father would always provide. Anything that Grandpa wanted, everyone did their best to get, as he was our top priority and our main concern. My mum learned to cook some of the more traditional food from the village, so that Grandpa would feel at home with us, but sadly, our best efforts couldn't stop the inevitable.

One night, Grandpa began to scream for my father and his entire body was shaking violently. My father told me to give him some water, while he phoned the doctor. Doctor Sam arrived at our house within twenty minutes; my father would have stressed the urgency of the situation. He ran into Grandpa's room with his briefcase and spent nearly two hours with him. Grandpa seemed to have calmed down a lot after this; he was barely moving at all now and the doctor spoke with my father in private.

My dad wasn't his usual self at all; he was exhausted and visibly concerned. That night was one of the longest of my life. I refused to go to bed because I wanted to be near my Grandpa at all times. I knew that was what he wanted too; although he couldn't say much, he repeated my name often. I would move my hand a bit to remind him that I was there and could hear his calls. Gradually, Grandpa's calls became less frequent. We fell asleep on the chairs by Grandpa, both holding one of his hands.

We both woke up at around 5am. It was already bright outside with the sun beaming in through the windows. We looked at Grandpa; he was completely motionless but because we were so exhausted we didn't think the worst straight away. We even tried not to make any noise so that we didn't wake him. It didn't take too long for my father to realise that something was wrong; he leant over Grandpa's chest to check his heartbeat, but while we had fallen asleep he had passed away.

Seeing my dad screaming, for his father and for the man who had been a father to me from when I was few months old, was harrowing. Cold ran down my spine. I was confused. I was upset and lost. I didn't know how to react. The shouting woke my mother, who was sleeping downstairs because she also wanted to be close to Grandpa. She rushed into the room and began to cry. I still hadn't fully comprehended what was happening: Grandpa had appeared to have fully recovered or at least was on the mend. We all thought he would soon be well enough to return to the village where he was more at ease.

Doctor Sam came to the house and rushed to Grandpa. He came out of the room with my parents, looking defeated, and my Grandpa's death was confirmed. After watching Grandma Eyadorobor die in my earlier childhood, I still didn't fully understand death but I understood well enough that I wouldn't see Grandpa again. Brother Eugene and I cried, but the other members of the family were too young to understand what was happening and just stood there motionless - staring at us.

My siblings hadn't grown up with Grandpa in the same way that I had; they had only really seen him on the few occasions when they had come to the village before and after I had moved. Grandpa always used to give them traditional village gifts and would play outside and joke with us. I knew my siblings would also miss him a great deal, even if they hadn't known him for as long as I did. Almost instantly, I thought of my Grandma Titi. She hadn't been able to be with the man she loved in his final hours, and I knew that she would be heartbroken.

A relative drove to the village to inform Grandma Titi of what had happened and then to bring her to Warri to be with us all. It wasn't long before I heard a car on the drive and saw her emerge from it. She looked completely lost and she was screaming and crying loudly, pulling her hair and stamping the ground in frustration and with anger for the loss of her dear husband and for not being there in his last hours. No doubt, Grandma expected Grandpa to be fully cured and returned back to the village to be with her, but it was not to be. I went straight over to her and gave her a hug - she seemed to really appreciate that. Grandma Titi went quickly into the room where Grandpa was; I hadn't been allowed in because of my age.

I could hear Grandma Titi and my parents crying in the room where Grandpa was and they didn't emerge for a long time. When they did eventually come out, Grandma Titi called me over to her; I held her hand tightly and we tried our best to comfort each other. All we could say was that we were sorry; we mainly repeated that and did our best to be there for each other.

Grandma Titi had always been the bravest woman I knew, but she was completely devastated by the loss of Grandpa, her closest companion, her husband. He had always been there to look after her and she was there all the time to care for him, especially during the war when Grandpa did his best to keep all of us safe. She had known him since they were teenagers and they had loved each other ever since; I felt sad knowing that she would have to carry on without him. The day stretched out slowly in front of us and most of us hardly moved from the living room; no one knew what to say but none of us wanted to be alone either. If the phone rang, the maid was told to say that we were not at home, so eventually it stopped ringing.

My uncle helped my father to arrange for a coffin; when it arrived it was taken quickly into Grandpa's resting place. I remember that it was gold plated. My siblings and I weren't allowed to see what was happening because we were too young. I still managed to peek through a space in the door; I wanted to pay my respects to the man who had brought me up, but when I tried to go inside the room, my father screamed at me to leave. My Grandma Titi wanted me to be there; I was always by my Grandpa's side when I lived with them in the village and I wanted to be by his side for the last time.

I did as I was told, but I refused to move from outside the door. I looked on as the coffin was moved from the room to a van which was parked outside, ready to take him back to the village. This would be done at night, to avoid the villagers asking us too many questions, which we weren't ready to answer. His death had not been made public yet; my Grandma Titi was the only person from the village who knew that Grandpa had passed away.

The night eventually came and Grandma Titi went with my other relatives to bring the coffin to the village mortuary, which was within the local hospital. Grandpa's body was left there to rest, whilst the funeral arrangements were made. Soon after, people were to be informed of what had happened. My father remained in Warri to make the funeral arrangements. The next morning, more of us went to the village to deliver items for the burial ceremony. As soon as we arrived it was clear that the whole village knew.

There were large posters, which were located high across several main road billboards and key advertising points in the village: "Papa chief Kokoruwe's Funeral, Saturday from 10am." By the time we got to our home, it was absolute mayhem; there were over a hundred people outside and inside the place I had called home for most of my life. Many men and women were weeping loudly and the children were all quiet; many of them had known Grandpa very well. He was always kind to all of us. Most of the market and the shops were closed; I had never seen the village like that on a Saturday, ever before. I always knew that my Grandpa was well liked but this showed me that he was very much loved by a lot of people. On that day, the village stood still.

We didn't stay in the village for long because we had to return to the city, Warri, to finalise more funeral arrangements. When we returned, I noticed that my father had had all of his hair shaved off; this was the village custom for men when someone in the family died. I wasn't sure why, but it had always been a mark of respect. When I was that age I didn't even like to have my hair cut, never mind having it shaved off completely, but as a mark of respect to my Grandpa I didn't hesitate.

Many people from outside of the family shaved their heads too. Grandpa was important to a lot of people.

The burial was the worst part. It took place in the village and I could see that my father was trying to be brave, until he saw Grandma Titi, who was sobbing uncontrollably. My father loved his father the same way any son does, but he also had a lot for which he was ever thankful to him. Grandpa had sent him to England to be educated; he worked hard for years and years in order to afford to send him abroad for a better education and to give him better opportunities in life.

Many of our relatives and close friends were in the living room, where the coffin was placed on a table; it was draped in a white cotton cloth and several candles were placed around it. My father made sure that Grandpa had the best of everything for his funeral. He bought every kind of drink that he could and several animals such as cows, sheep, goats and chickens. It made me think of everything my grandparents had done, not so long ago, to celebrate my father's return to the village.

It was an established custom in the village to bury the owner of the house inside his property, so Grandpa was laid to rest in the centre of the living room, where he had spent most of his life after the war. The floor was literally dug out. It was normally just plain soil with no concrete, carpets or any other coverings. The indoor grave was as deep as the grave diggers could dig. I didn't see how deep but it was usually so deep that one wouldn't notice anything different once it was covered and made as smooth as before the burial.

I couldn't stop crying when I realised that Grandpa really would be gone forever. He was being buried before my very eyes in the room where he had often chatted and joked with me when I lived with him. I remembered losing Grandma Eyadorobor as a child immediately after the war, and I cried for her and Grandpa.

Grandma Titi was the strongest out of all of us during the burial; she held my hand and reassured me that there was no need to cry now, as Grandpa was with God in a much better place where he couldn't feel pain any more. She had an admirable strong faith and this encouraged me to try and think more positively about Grandpa. He had gone to God for a better future.

During the burial ceremony, I got the chance to see many of my old friends whom I hadn't seen properly for some time. I missed the days when I could spend all day playing in the village with them; now I had a lot of responsibilities and expectations of me. Things weren't the same any more. My friends knew how close I was to my Grandpa, so they were a great comfort to be with at the time. They gave me a hug after the ceremony and I also knew that they would help Grandma Titi in any way that they could now that Grandpa was gone; just like they supported Grandpa and Grandma Titi when I left the village for the city.

It was still sad to think that Grandpa wouldn't be there when I visited the village at weekends and during the holidays. He had taught me so much: how to cultivate the farm, trap animals, ride a bike and even how to use a shot gun. He taught me things that no one else would have, and they would remain with me for the rest of my life. Many people from the village came to offer me their condolences and I really appreciated that; it was a comfort to know that people were wishing me the best and that they really cared.

Chapter Nine

Murder in The City

After a few days we all had to return to Warri. I felt really worried about leaving Grandma Titi, but I promised her that I would be back to visit her soon. It was a difficult journey home; throughout, we were all thinking about Grandpa and how much we would miss him - none of us spoke. When we did get there, the maid showed us that we had received gifts from well-wishers. I found this astonishing; it was amazing to think that Grandpa had all these friends in the city as well as in the village. It must have been a great comfort to my father that his friends and work colleagues had shown their support for his loss.

We all remained at home for a few days after our return to Warri, but did our best to carry on as normal. Nonetheless, it didn't feel like much time had passed before my parents were back in work and we were back in school. I didn't feel happy about returning to school. I had been in Warri nearly eight months but I hadn't made any good friends that I could look forward to seeing every day. I missed my friends in the village and the freedom to play outside freely. There were no woodlands or proper forests nearby where I could walk, pick mushrooms and fruit, or just generally play around. In Warri there were also a lot more cars and motorbikes and the smell of the fumes wasn't something that I was accustomed to. With the roads being so busy, it meant that the sound of beeping horns was constant; there was no peace. There always seemed to be music playing from somewhere, day and night, which made getting to sleep extremely difficult. We were luckier than most; our home was located in one of the more secluded parts of the city, so we were afforded some peaceful respites. Eventually even this proved to be a danger to us.

In the middle of an ordinary night, I heard three very loud bangs and I realised almost instantly that these bangs had come from gunshots. Fortunately this set off the burglar alarm in the house next door, which woke my entire household straightaway. My cousin, Isaac, was the first one to come to his senses; he switched on the lights in our home and managed to see a burglar climbing out of a side window. He was even brave enough to try and chase him, but looking back, I'm glad he didn't catch up with a burglar who was armed with a loaded gun. Although it was only the early hours of the morning, the adults stayed up with us until the morning. It was around an hour before the police arrived, by which time the burglar was long gone. They questioned our neighbours to see if they had noticed anything which could identify the burglar, but they hadn't seen anything. Our family had only seen a glimpse of the burglar from the back, which wasn't sufficient to identify the individual.

We learnt later that the security guard in our neighbour's house had been shot dead. This scared us.

It was a shock for me. In the village, we always left our doors and windows open and there was no fear of something like this, partly because there were no possessions to steal. Most people had the same things in their homes. More importantly than that the village was like a big family, we all knew and trusted each other, and knew we were safe in our homes. The city was different. It was much bigger, and there were many people from different cultural and religious backgrounds. Some people were very rich and had important possessions, while others were rather poor and desperate for money to feed themselves and possible their family members. Trust was a difficult thing to build in such circumstances. There were also numerous different languages which were spoken; Urobo, Yoruba and Fulani were the most popular. Around half of the population in Warri were Christians and the other half were Muslims, which made integration very difficult.

If I had been given the choice, I would have returned to the village where I would have felt much safer. There was no risk there that one person would deliberately cause harm to another and, if it was not for the terrible war that took so many lives, I would have thought people could only die from illness and not deliberately at the hands of one another.

I became more worried about returning to school in the city after Grandpa's burial; I felt self-conscious about my shaved head and I wished that my hair would grow back quickly. In the village everyone knew Grandpa and had their heads shaved as well, but in the city this wasn't common practice. I would be the odd one out, but, eventually I didn't care much; it was done for my dear grandpa. Nonetheless, my parents prepared me for my return to school. I think they knew I was unhappy but I didn't voice my issues to them. It still wasn't as easy for me to express my feelings in English; I understood the words but they didn't hold the same meaning for me and always felt very artificial. When I returned, I was even more quiet than usual. At school lunch time, I would often run the short distance to my house for food or just to get away from the school and then return for classes afterwards. Sometimes I didn't return, instead I walked around the shops or simply stayed out of the sight of my parents and teachers. The school wasn't especially concerned with absences, and teachers, if they did ask, wouldn't do more than enquire uninterestedly as to where you had been.

After a while, I had to become more vigilant. I missed so many classes that the teachers raised the issue with my father. He became steadily stricter with all of us. If Dad became angry, he would whip us with his belt as a form of punishment - we could be whipped for failing exams, ignoring our homework or staying out with our friends longer than we had been permitted to, even if these friends were next door. Education should have been our top priority. Every evening we had to show Dad the work we had done; he even purchased books for our teachers to write comments in concerning our work and general behaviour. If the comments were particularly bad, Dad would wait until Mum had gone out before whipping us. He preferred not to do so in front of her; she would argue with him and do all she could to stop Dad getting hold of us for our punishment. Mum would also get extremely upset over this harsh treatment of us. I had grown up in a village, so I was more accustomed to pain than my siblings were. My little sister Edore was especially terrified of being punished by Dad; she would often begin to cry as soon as she saw the belt ready and before she felt it. This annoyed my father even more. The number of whips we received would depend largely upon how bad our performance in school had been. When it was my turn, I didn't hesitate to accept my punishment. My father began to see that this wasn't going to get me to change so he began to try a new tactic. He would shout at me and ensure that I promised to work harder. Dad knew I had been brought up to keep my promises; not doing so would make me a weak child. He found this to be more effective as I didn't want to be called a weak child by anyone, for Grandpa has always instilled in me that I was a strong individual.

Chapter Ten

Killings by The School

I began to put in more effort into my work and started to ensure I was at all of my afternoon lessons after the lunch break. The events of an afternoon lesson on one Friday made my father really regret enrolling us in that school. Just as a lesson was about to finish, we could see people crowding around the army barracks, which were next to the school. Everyone was trying to see out of the classroom window and we were speculating among ourselves as to what was happening.

When the school bell went to signal the end of lessons and the school day, the teachers couldn't stop us from running outside to see what was actually going on. We ran towards the barracks. There was a huge field in front of the army base, where the soldiers often marched; in the field were several oil barrels which were filled with sand and there were long poles concreted inside them. No one knew what was supposed to be happening and there were no attempts by the army to cover anything up. I thought at first that it would be a sort of skills demonstration from the soldiers, as there were over a hundred of them lined up in their full uniform. Then I saw blindfolded men being dragged into the field from a nearby army van. They were then tied around the posts.

I was still puzzled, even when a priest arrived and spoke to the men who had been tied up; I didn't comprehend what was about to happen. I thought it was maybe some sort of drama show was taking place. I became bored as time went on but the large crowd was screaming and shouting. I panicked and became anxious; I realised then that it wouldn't be a practice drill or drama show, it was taking too long and I would have the opportunity to see one again another time. For now, I wanted to get home and enjoy the weekend. I said goodbye to the people who had gathered from my class and started walking away. Then I heard the gunshots. I turned around to see three bodies slumped around the posts - they had been tied there and prepared for execution, for whatever crimes they had committed. I peeked through the crowds and for a few moments I couldn't register what I was seeing. Just like that, their lives had been taken from them.

Afterwards I learned more about what these men had done, which warranted that kind of punishment. They were thieves who had killed someone during a recent burglary, which had gone wrong. I wasn't sure that taking their lives in exchange for another was right. Even when I thought of the attempted burglary at the house next to ours the other day, I still didn't think that killing the criminals was the right solution. I couldn't help wondering if one of these men had been involved in the next door's burglary, where the security guard was murdered.

I heard the adults around me saying that these men hadn't been given a trial, so even if killing them was the price to be paid, how did the army know they had killed the right people? I prayed and prayed that these men were at least guilty of the crime they had been accused of, even if the punishment was severe. I couldn't understand the justice system and I wanted more than ever to return to my peaceful village.

My parents found out soon later on and they were shocked and furious in equal measure. They couldn't believe that this had been carried out in front of young schoolchildren, without a thought for how the children would feel emotionally. The events of that day dominated my thoughts whenever I was in school after that, making it very difficult for me to sleep and to concentrate. Now and then I had nightmares about it, which kept me awake.

Whenever I was in lessons, I could see the faces of the people who had been shot dead, the blood pouring from their bodies after the multiple bullets. I could see some faces in the crowd; some of them had looked excited. I thought of how the families of those who had been killed would feel: if it had been a member of my family, I would have been ashamed of them for their crime, but, I know I wouldn't have wanted them to die for it. Even worse, being publicly executed was a very traumatic experience to witness when we were only children. I supposed many other children had nightmares too and many were too sick to come to school during the next few days.

My father became very understanding for a while and he stopped punishing us when we didn't perform adequately at school; after all, we could only try our best and if we had known the answers to the questions one hundred percent, we would have given the answers one hundred percent accurately, but it wasn't possible to recall the full details of the lessons, or, if I had made mistakes in my homework. Soon after the event, my father was transferred to the staff quarters at Petroleum Training Institute, Effurun.

Chapter Eleven

The Deadly Storm

Effurun was a district in the north of Warri and it was slightly more modern, as it was located on the outskirts of the city. Many of the villagers lived in poverty, which was extremely prevalent in the more crowded towns. The lucky ones were able to travel by bicycle but, most had to walk barefoot. Our home in the staff estate was one of the most modern buildings in the entire district, it had been newly built and we were amongst the first families to live in it. There were armed security guards, who patrolled the complex twenty-four hours a day; not that this was necessary for our security – the property was surrounded by a twelve- foot tall barbed wire fence. My father's office was in the complex, along with a swimming pool, football pitch, tennis court, cinema, restaurant and bar. These facilities were exclusively for the use of the employees and their families, and couldn't be accessed by anyone else, except in exceptional situations, when guests of employees would be allowed to use them.

We had been to view the house and complex before my father had accepted the offer of living there, and we had been impressed. My siblings and Mum couldn't wait to live there, and I also shared in their excitement. The complex had a power supply which was separate to the one which the rest of the town ran from; this meant that if there was a storm or an issue with the main supply, we and those who had their own generators would be the only ones to have electricity. I liked it, more so than all the other reasons, because it was closer to Grandma Titi's village. I was pleased that I would be able to see more of her, and also that it would be easier for her to come and visit us, even though she preferred village life to a city one.

Our home was a bungalow with four bedrooms and three bathrooms. My mother was pleased because the living room and kitchen were much bigger than they had been at our old house, which meant it would be much easier for her to entertain guests in our home. The garden was large, but still needed some work. The whole family worked together to make it look nice and more like a home, by planting flowers around the boundaries of the property to create our own mini fence. There were some trees too, which managed to hide part of the building completely, giving us much needed shade. Behind the house has an annexe, which acted as guest-quarters and a place which our caretakers occupied. It had three bedrooms, a bath/shower room and a kitchen. On the complex there were around twenty detached houses, in different shapes and styles. For the lower ranking members of staff there were multi-story properties, containing modern and spacious flats.

Our new home was much further from my school, and this was what finally encouraged my father to apply for a transfer. He had also been displeased about the quality of the homework at my previous school; he felt that we were never given enough, which meant (to him) that it was an academically poor school. Dad didn't think it would prepare us for our higher education examinations, that we needed to pass in order to progress to a college and then to university. I think we were all glad to see the back of that school after the terrible things which we had seen there, and even before that I had never truly settled in. I looked forward to the opportunity of a fresh start, where I would hopefully make some new friends.

My father's work colleague lived opposite our home, with his wife and two daughters. Edore quickly became friends with his daughters, Henrietta and Josephine. I always found it difficult to tell them apart; even though Jo was a year older, they both always wore matching outfits and they had the same haircut. They always wore lovely jewellery, like simple earrings and delicate necklaces. Their personalities couldn't have been more different; Henrietta was serious but Jo was always laughing and more playful. Sometimes they would come to our house with Edore so that they could play games and listen to music together. The moment Edore returned from school, she was on the phone to Jo and Henrietta; luckily my father's work paid the phone bills so we didn't have to panic about the cost when Edore had spent three hours on it. We moved in during the half term holidays; my father informed my teachers of the transfer but I hadn't bothered to tell my classmates as there was no one there whom I would miss.

I had found my sister's friends difficult to get along with sometimes; I didn't know many girls in the village, and I found them difficult to relate to. They didn't like football, and they seemed to spend their days getting ready for parties or to go to the shops. They made me shy so quite often when they came over, I would just stay in my room. I knew that Jo would often ask my sister where I was, which would result in lots of teasing and joking about how Jo loved me. I would often lock my bedroom door so that the girls couldn't come in. There were occasions when they would climb through my bedroom window! When they managed this, I was often forced to give up, leave my hiding place and come outside to play games with everyone - I had to admire their determination.

Some of the biggest differences between village and city life were birthdays. There were no birthday cards or presents, like those which were handed out in the city, they were considered as being pointless luxuries. Many people in the village forgot their birthdays entirely, along with their age. In the city it was different; they could afford to spend the money on cake and entertainment if they wanted to. My father had drawn the short straw with birthdays. My birthday was on December 21st, Edore's was on December 24th, and then it was Christmas Day. It was so expensive to buy us birthday gifts and followed by Christmas gifts for everybody a day later! He had tried to get us one gift for Christmas and birthdays, but we refused to let Dad have a minute's rest until we had separate presents for both occasions after all it was not our decision to be born in December or near to Christmas Day.

By the time our birthdays came around I had been in the city for almost a year, and I hadn't really tried to make friends or meet new people. I still missed my old friends in the village, and the woodland where we could all play freely. This meant that when my sister and I celebrated our birthdays together, I had no friends to invite to the party. We had relatives and family friends who came with their children, but I didn't know them well enough to be comfortable playing and celebrating my birthday with them. Most of the people who attended the party were girls; this made it difficult for me to enjoy it, especially with Jo and Hetty trying to wind me up. In preparation for the party, my parents took us to the tailor for new clothes and we were bought new shoes. There was no expense spared on the food, we had special fried jollof rice with chicken and other meats, and there were bottles of fizzy drinks for the children. The adults had a choice of lagers, spirits and wine, which meant that they would often get very tipsy and sing and dance with whoever was on the dance floor.

I was still very shy and made every excuse that I could come up with, to go to my room. My mum noticed this and would come upstairs to get me; as it was my party, I was expected to be present at all times and show my face. When I had come back down at Mum's request, she would try to pull me on to the dance floor, which made me feel really nervous and shy. My sister's friends would often try to dance with me; if I tried to run away from them, they would chase me so I was unable to avoid joining in with the dancing and celebrations for very long. I couldn't wait for it to be over, and as soon as the guests had left, I looked forward to an early night. My parents could tell that I hadn't really enjoyed myself, and Edore made sure she told them that I wouldn't dance and join in with the other children. I would always feel guilty after my birthdays; my parents went to a lot of trouble to organise them, but, I never felt comfortable enough to enjoy the celebrations the same way that everyone else did.

At the beginning of the school term, Dad drove Edore and I to have a look at our new school, Orerokpe Grammar School. It was around forty minutes from our new home in Effurun, and I felt bad that my father would have to make this journey every day. I realised after the first day that Dad had other ideas; he instructed his driver to take us to and from school on his behalf, only occasionally when Dad wasn't busy did he elect to either drop us at school or to pick us up himself.

Although we had only come to look around so that my father could be assured it was a safer environment than our previous school, Edore and I noticed the differences for ourselves. There were no army barracks nearby; since the incident at my previous school I no longer thought they were interesting, they invariably made me nervous. There were enough tables and chairs for all of the teachers and pupils, unlike before. The school uniform was smart; girls wore green skirts and white shirts, and boys wore green shorts and white shirts. They were all smiling! As we walked in and out of the classrooms, the teacher would introduce us, "This is Brian Kokoruwe. This is his sister, Edore Kokoruwe. They are going to join us from tomorrow." I smiled back at them and waved slightly as we left the classrooms for the next ones.

Unlike previous schools, the new school had glass coverings on the windows. This confirmed to us that the pupils were well behaved, as they had looked after the glass and not smashed it. There were no doors in the classrooms, only the Headmaster's and teachers' offices had doors that could be locked. The classrooms didn't have carpets, instead there were cement floors which were regularly swept with broomsticks - there were no Hoovers then.

Even though lessons were taking place while we toured the school, there were pupils who were cutting the grass in the school grounds - I couldn't work out why they would be doing that when there was important information to be learnt. I nudged my sister and gestured towards the pupils who were outside. She shrugged her shoulders at me, but then suggested that they could be getting punished for bad behaviour; this suggestion made a lot of sense. Neither of us wanted to end up cutting the grass or doing cleaning duties, so we were even quieter as we carried on our tour.

The teachers were somewhat concerned about how far away we lived, particularly with lessons commencing at 8.30am. My father was very committed to making sure we got the best out of our education, and he assured them that the distance wouldn't be an issue. We met the headmaster, who reassured my father that this would be the best school to send his children to; this seemed to please my father and reassured him that his choice had been for the best.

We decided not to bring up the issue of pupils cutting the grass as a form of punishment, because I didn't think Dad would want to hear that we could be treated like that. Edore and I expressed our enthusiasm about the school, and the fact that it was a much nicer environment than our previous one. This made the headmaster smile. When we left his office, all of the children who had been cutting the grass had disappeared; Edore and I thought they had been told to remain out of sight until Dad left, so that there would be no potential objections raised on his part about the school's standards. We left, with the reassurance that we would be returning the next day as fully enrolled pupils. When we got back home, Dad quickly had the tailor measure us up and he kitted us out in the green and white uniform of Orerokpe Grammar School.

I enjoyed the first drive back from Orerokpe; unlike the journey there I wasn't half asleep, I even noticed the bridge that I had heard people speaking about. There were no barriers on it, and it was just wide enough for two cars to pass simultaneously, which often made it dangerous to cross. If a car or lorry was very large, or, if the vehicle was slightly off their side of the road, it resulted in accidents. Sometimes they would collide against each other, causing external damage, but occasionally the consequences were far worse; cars would fall into the river, which resulted in people being trapped inside them and drowning!

According to local legend, at night time good spirits would cross the bridge. Some people said that they were the spirits of those who had died there, searching ceaselessly for their eternal resting place. For this reason, the local government refused to pay for barriers to be built, because it was frightened that it would incur the wrath of the spirits who resided there. Absolute nonsense! Newly built barriers could hardly have been expected to hamper the movements of spirits, and that was even assuming that they existed in the first place. It was a lot more likely that the local government had wasted its budget and was using the superstitions of the Nigerian people to cover itself.

Many poor villagers would stand on the road beside the bridge, selling what they had produced on their farm as cars and trucks slowed down to cross the bridge. The area around the bridge became like a market. They sold everything from dry fish (fresh fish that that been dried in the sun) to firewood, avocados, oranges, corns, groundnuts, and freshly caught fish. It all depended on the season.

Dad usually stopped to get us something to eat or something to take home for dinner. Edore, who was usually determined to have something to eat, would fall asleep as soon as we got into the car, her hand still clutching the food item. We had to wake up early each morning for the long journey to school and we got tired on the way back home! Dad would sometimes try to sing and tell us stories, or ask us questions about what had happened in school that day, to stop us falling asleep and then leaving him with no one to hold a conversation with on the journey back home. Although it was interesting, the road conditions were terrible. Dad would often have to veer across the road to avoid large potholes, which could have caused damage to his company car.

Once we had settled into a routine, driving to and from school was no longer interesting; leaving early and getting home extremely late was tiring for us, and it was beginning to affect my concentration. Edore was doing better than me in some subjects, and Dad wasn't pleased about it. In order to improve our grades, he decided to begin paying the teachers to provide us with extra tuition at home. Edore and I weren't keen on the idea – we were tired and doing our best to concentrate in school, to then come home and do the same thing again wasn't fun. Monsieur Fabrice was our French teacher, and even though his French was perfect, his English wasn't at a much better standard than mine. If we asked him a question in English, he would often struggle to answer, and it wasn't long after this that Dad began to question the academic ability of the other teachers.

One morning, when we had been at school for several weeks, the weather took a very alarming turn. The rain was especially heavy – although rain in itself isn't uncommon in Nigeria. Even though it was 11am, it was still strangely dark. The usual refreshing breeze had been replaced with something much more aggressive, like a hurricane. Empty cans and bits of plastic objects could be seen flying through the air and it was beginning to get quite eerie. All of a sudden, the sky was lit up by a flash of lightning, and the sound of thunder began to fill the classroom. Many of us began to panic; our English teacher urged us to remain calm but we could hear in his voice that he was just as alarmed and panicky as us children. The thunder continued, and seemed to be getting closer by the minute. Everyone seemed to panic all at once; there was a sudden mad rush to hide under the desks, with our hands covering our ears. I think we hid for around ten minutes before the storm had stopped. The teacher, who had also sought refuge under a desk, regained his authority and told us to get out from under the classroom furniture.

I looked outside and couldn't believe it; the sunshine had returned and there was hardly any trace of the storm, except from some wetness on the surface of the grass. I was amazed at how quickly the weather had altered. We had all lost interest in the lesson, so our tutor allowed us to take an earlier lunch break. I bumped into Edore and we both agreed how scary the experience had been. We had just begun to calm down when we heard screaming. We looked and saw pupils from the other side of the school running towards the playground. When I looked up, I saw that the large oak tree beside the other classrooms had been torn in two by the storm; one half had fallen into the building.

Someone screamed: "My friend! My friend! He's been killed!"

I felt sick. It turned out that during the thunder, lightning had struck one of the pupils and killed him, even though he was in the middle of classroom. Everyone else in the room had been physically unharmed. The ambulance arrived quickly so that the lifeless body could be promptly removed from the school grounds. None of us could understand how something like this could happen. It had seemed like such a normal day, and then a cruel, random chain of events had robbed an innocent young boy of his life. It seemed so unlikely that it could even have happened – some people began to say that the boy had been cursed by a witch. Although this may seem like a strange connection to make, it was the only way that some could make sense out of it.

The whole school was sent to the assembly hall, where we waited anxiously for the arrival of the headmaster. There were so many of us crammed into the hall; I could still hear sobbing, and many pupils were in a state of extreme panic, because of what we had witnessed.

"Today you have all witnessed something truly terrible, the death of a fellow pupil. Until his entire family have been informed, we cannot disclose his identity. Tomorrow will be a day of mourning, which means that all lessons will be cancelled until Monday - when we will expect you in at the usual time. School has finished for today; you may go home."

Our teacher had to arrange a taxi to get us home, and fortunately we arrived there in time to catch Dad as he was leaving to get us. There was no telephone to contact families in those days. Edore told Dad what had happened, but I preferred to stay quiet. I wasn't really listening to what mistresses, but a lady being in a relationship prior to marriage was unthinkable. Women were expected to remain faithful, while men could break their marriage vows if they saw fit. Fortunately, my father had spent a considerable amount of time away from these values pertaining to female education. He believed that all his children, regardless of their gender, were entitled to the best education that he could provide them with. So, with this in mind, he withdrew us from Oreropke Grammar School.

Dad managed to get me an opportunity to sit the common entrance examination for Ughelli Government College, one of the best schools in the country at that time. It was an all-boys school, and located around *km from our city. Ughelli is a renowned market town where you could purchase almost any kind of produce; from prawns to shark fish or baby *es to traditional clothing for native rulers or smart suits for business *le.

*knew the town well; when we drove from Warri to visit my parents in Iluelogbo, we always used to drive through Ughelli town. *ould stop to go shopping, often for presents for my grandparents, *which they couldn't get as easily in their small village. However *pping wasn't the first thing people noticed about Ughelli; the *was always terrible. Most of the market traders had no shops, or

was being said, I saw how my Dad's face changed from shock to ang
because that innocent boy could easily have been either of his child
Mum came running outside when she saw us all gathered at the fro
the house; Edore once again explained what had happened. Mum
to cry, while she held us tightly, thanking God that her children we

Dad wasted no time changing our schooling arrangements.
been concerned about the distance we had to travel every
prospects of pupils from Oreropke advancing to higher educatic
impossible but very low in those days. This displeased my fa
before my sister's account of the incident that had occur
become worried about us continuing at that school.

In Nigeria, girls generally had two options; to be marr
they could become housewives, or to sell their father's
markets until a husband was found. It was extremely rare
have a better job than a man, and they had to accept
inferior place in society. Women were not supposed
men, and this was probably why most of them didn't
school - anything they learned was unlikely to be o'
household or at the farm.

Most men viewed it as their duty to look after wc
that they would a child. Men were allowed

particular areas where they would sell their goods; instead they carried their goods in giant aluminium bowls or basins on their heads, as they strolled from one place to another trying to sell what they were carrying.

Drivers would see the traders, and stop their cars to purchase the items that they wanted, but if a motorist stopped to buy produce from one trader, many other traders would often come to the car in the hopes of selling their produce too. Traders were unconcerned with their own safety when they sold their products; they would run carelessly towards moving traffic, just so they could sell produce which would enable them to feed themselves and or their family that day.

Taxi drivers were also a cause of this terrible traffic. They would stop traffic to pick up extra passengers, and would often fill vehicles with far more people than they were built to carry. There were also stray animals; goats, sheep, chicken and even cows could be seen roaming the streets in search of food. Most drivers would be very cautious if there were animals nearby because they knew they were likely to be the lost property of a poor villager, who would need to sell them at some points to make a living. There were also the heavy goods vehicles; the lorries that were over-filled with far more products than they were built to carry. They struggled with driving along the roads and were often crawling at a snail's pace through the town; causing damage to the roads and therefore even more traffic jams.

Despite all of this, Ughelli conditions were much better than those of the villages in certain respects. Unlike in the villages, where most of the houses were built of clay with thatch roofs, the houses in Ughelli were detached and well-built. Most of them were privately owned, but, some did belong to the government. Each house had a private driveway, with various fruits and vegetables growing in the area around it, largely for decorative purposes, rather than for the fruits which were left to fall and rot on the ground around many of the houses.

In Ughelli you would always notice Government College pupils; they wore white shirts and brown trousers, with a distinctive red and yellow badge. Edore and I were excited and nervous at the prospect of transferring to better schools; although I was looking forward to the prospect of attending such a good school, again I wouldn't know anyone there. My brother Eugene was a great help to me; he had studied there briefly and reassured me that he had friends there who would look after me. Despite his helpful reassurance and advice, I was still getting more worried by the day. If I was unable to pass the exam, I was worried that I would be a failure to my parents and the rest of my family. The pressure increased when I found out that if I passed the exam to attain a place at

Ughelli, I would be attending as a boarding pupil. Now I would have to face the worry of potentially leaving the family that I had only just begun to know, to join another unfamiliar environment.

Edore, on the other hand, wouldn't be sent away from home. She was expected to sit exams for the equally prestigious Our Lady's High School; it was a very strict Catholic school for girls, but as it was only a few miles away from home, there would be no need for her to board there. My dad did his best to encourage me, but most of the time it resulted in making me more nervous. He informed me, with the intention of filling me with pride, that I would sit exams in English, maths and general knowledge; there were only sixty places available, with over three hundred applicants, but I think I would have preferred not to know that at the time.

My dad had taken care to impress upon me the importance of the opportunity he had secured for me; I was still young, but I would have to take full responsibility for my own actions now. The prospect was a frightening one, but I knew that I would make everyone so proud if I succeeded. In the weeks running up to my exams Dad would often come home from work early, and he would bring extra books to prepare us for our exams. Even though it was half term, and all my friends were outside enjoying their free time, I was expected to use the time to stay in and study. Dad even began asking me questions before he left for work, at 5am in the morning! He would wake me up and quiz me on my arithmetic knowledge when I could barely keep my eyes open. Dad had made strict study plans for Edore and I, as soon as we arrived home from school we ate and then started studying. Whatever lessons we had had in the day would determine what we studied in the evening; if we'd had French and maths in school, then that was what we had to study when we came home. Although the repetition was boring, I found that I was taking in much more information and my concentration at school began to improve.

Luckily for us, Dad knew what he was doing. He had completed a Masters degree, and part of his job involved tutoring university undergraduates. Even though I was pleased to have the opportunity to make my family proud, I still sometimes felt sad that I was missing out on my freedom. How my life was now couldn't be more different from the time I spent living in the village with my grandparents, where things had been so much simpler. Sometimes I used to wonder what it would have been like for me if I had never left.

The night before the exam was terrible. I could hardly sleep at all, because I knew how difficult the questions were going to be; I was worried that I would begin the exam and panic, and be left unable to answer a single question. If I failed, then the weeks of studying and preparation would have all been for nothing.

I remember very little of the morning of the exam, just a constant feeling of anxiety. Eugene came with me and my parents; he was able to give me lots of useful tips – but I knew that when I went in it would all be up to me. I could see my own nervousness reflected in Dad's face when he gave me a quick hug before I entered the exam hall.

"You are now expected to put your pens down and shut your answer booklets."

When I heard those words, I felt as if I was able to breathe for the first time in weeks. I wanted to run out of the exam hall, but there were too many other pupils in the way, who probably wished that they could do the same. I had to push my way through an endless crowd of pupils and their family members before I could find my own. Once I found them, they immediately began to question me on the exam. I told them that I had answered all the questions and done the best that I could.

All that was left to do now was to wait. We were all nervous, and no one knew what to say. Dad eventually got sick of waiting and told us that he was going to go and find out the results himself. I was just glad that someone was doing something other than staring at the floor. He didn't return for a further forty minutes, but by looking at his face it was clear that he had seen the results. He was smiling wider than I had ever seen anyone smile and his eyes had lost the look of nervousness, which had been so dominant this morning. He came over, and confirmed that I had passed and gave me a massive hug. I still needed to see the results for myself, so Dad agreed to take me to where they were displayed. They had been posted on a notice board, which was barely visible through the crowd of people. There were some extremely happy faces, unable to contain their excitement, but there were many with more disappointed faces, tears rolling down their cheeks, as they could not contain their sadness.

When I looked at the notice board, I was given a further surprise, out of the hundreds of candidates I had come fourth. I was extremely proud that I was able to make my family proud with my efforts, but there were still worries I had, which were dampening what should have been a happy occasion. I wondered how my day to day life would be from now on, like where I would store my personal belongings, or how I would be woken up in the morning. I also didn't know how things would be arranged when it came to seeing my family – if there were limits on how often they could visit, and if I would be allowed to go home every weekend. These worries and many other concerns were on my mind on the journey home. I was so preoccupied with my thoughts that I barely noticed when we got there, as I had fallen asleep.

Eugene who had returned home when the Common Entrance Examination started, was waiting for us on the driveway, and the car had barely stopped before he had raced over to open the car door and asked how the exams had gone. Before I could reply, Mum told him that I had come fourth out of all the candidates. Eugene lifted me out of the car and spun me around in a tight hug; he was shouting his congratulations which soon attracted the attention of other people. Our driveway quickly began to fill up with a crowd of people who came over to congratulate me and my family on the good news. I looked around me at all the smiling faces, and I felt proud that I had been able to bring joy to these people through my hard work.

One month before school began, my parents received a list of all the items I would need to have before starting school. It took several shopping trips to obtain the stationery, bags, shoes and sportswear that I needed; I also had to be taken for a fitting with a tailor for my school uniform. Although I was busy preparing for my new school, when I had time to think about my future I was overcome with worries.

My relationship with my friends also changed. Many of them had congratulated me – and had seemed genuinely pleased – but others became distant from me when they heard my good news. They didn't invite me out with them as often as they used to, perhaps because they knew I was busy with preparing for school or because they were jealous of the opportunity that I had been given. The isolation only added to the worries that I had.

The day before school began, Mum helped me to pack my luggage. I had two suitcases; one contained my clothes, shoes and school essentials, the other was full of my favourite food items – biscuits, powdered milk, condensed milk, chocolate drink mixture and sugar, in case the school didn't have them. I was staring into the suitcases, which contained everything from home that I would be able to take with me, and I felt a hand touch my shoulder. Instinctively, I knew that it was my mum.

"Don't worry about anything son, you're going to be just fine. We will come to visit you as often as we can, and you can come home regularly if that is what you want to do."

I looked up at Mum's face. I saw the tears rolling down her cheeks. This brought tears to my eyes too and I held Mum tighter. I didn't want to let go. My mother's kind words reassured me momentarily, but then I realised the significance of what she was saying; from now on I would not see my parents 'regularly' and rarely be able to speak with them on a daily basis. The rest of the time I would be alone in an unfamiliar environment.

We had a final family meal together before I left, although no one had much to say. I didn't feel like eating very much, even though I was unsure when I would next have my mum's cooking. Before long we were standing on the drive, loading the car; it seemed strange that not long ago we had all been standing here celebrating and now the mood was much more solemn. Edore and Ben also came with my parents to bring me to school. They were joking with me on the journey; Edore threatened to eat all of my favourite food and Ben said he was going to use my bedroom. I was protective over my favourite food, and the thought of someone snooping around in my private space, in my room, annoyed me – but I knew that I would even miss my siblings teasing me; our fights, joys and love.

"We're here," Dad's words interrupted the joking between my siblings and I.

I looked out of the car window and saw a sign *'Welcome to Government College, Ughelli'*. This reminded me of when I came to the College for the Common Entrance Examinations. We approached a large entrance gate, but before we could pass through an old man suddenly appeared.

"What brings you here?" he asked bluntly, as he approached my Dad's window.

He had an unkempt appearance, and I could see when he spoke that most of his teeth were missing. For some reason, he made me feel nervous.

"I am here to take my son, Brian, to school; he begins studying here tomorrow."

"House name?"

"Orerokpe House. Would you mind pointing me in the right direction?"

Coincidentally, the name of my boarding House was the same name as the school, which I had just left for this new one.

"That way on the left," and with those blunt instructions he left just as quickly as he had appeared.

I hoped that not everyone at the college had such bad manners. All the buildings which we drove past were identically built but in different colours. Their appearance was similar to a typical hotel. I was also pleased when I discovered that the building that I would be living in was the closest to the classrooms.

We parked the car right outside and as I got out, I noticed that several pupils were peeking out of the windows and staring at us. Dad walked confidently over to the main building, while I followed. He knocked on the 'Head Prefect' door; he had only just pulled his hand back before it swung open to reveal a senior pupil.

"Good afternoon, sir."

"Hello Bobby, how are you?"

"I'm fine, thank you, sir. How can I help you?"

"This is my son, Brian. I spoke with your father and he said that I can trust you to look after my son. I hope that you will act like he is your little brother; make sure he studies, does his homework on time and doesn't get picked on by other children."

While my father gave his instructions, Bobby was nodding and seemed to be taking every word extremely seriously.

"You can rely on me to look after Brian, sir," Bobby spoke with confidence and signalled for me to walk towards him. He shook my hand and held me near him; keeping me away from my dad. I suppose he was just starting to accept responsibility for me in the presence of my dad.

I felt as though he was likely to be trustworthy; the school would presumably not give him this position of authority if he was unworthy of it.

"How are you, Brian? If you and your dad would like to follow me, I can show you where you will sleep and your personal storage for your things."

Dad and I followed Bobby into the main building, while everyone else waited in the car. When Bobby opened the door, I was instantly disappointed. There seemed to be endless rows of bunk beds and they weren't spaced far apart enough. There was a concrete floor – no carpets – and I couldn't see a fridge; from the oppressive heat I also deduced that there was no air conditioning. This wasn't what I had expected the living conditions to be like.

I looked around the room and began to notice some of my fellow pupils; most of them appeared to be studying, but some were just staring absent-mindedly at the ceiling.

"This is Ugochukuka, Jim, Simon, Frankie, David, Isaac…" Bobby continued to reel off names, while I murmured my hellos to the sea of unfamiliar faces.

We eventually reached the end of the dormitory where the toilet facilities were located. The disappointment continued; there was no mirror, toilet paper or keys to lock the doors. Immediately next to the toilets were rows of shower cubicles but I couldn't see any soap. I happened to look at the taps, but there were no symbols on them to indicate which ones were hot and which ones were cold.

Bobby seemed to read my mind, because he turned to me and said, "All of the taps are cold here, you will get used to it in no time."

I wondered how likely my dad was to reconsider boarding school. I peered up at him cautiously and decided that would be unlikely; I could see from his face that he didn't share my disdain for my surroundings. From what I'd seen, I made my mind up that I wasn't likely to be fond of the food either.

When we finished our tour of the dorm, we began the walk back to my mum and siblings. I could tell that Edore and Ben were glad they wouldn't be attending a boarding school and that they would finish school and return home to their own rooms and family. If I were in their position, I would feel the same way. I knew that Mum didn't particularly want me to go; she had already had to say goodbye to me once when I was only three months old. Although she had spoken with Dad about her reservations, Dad had done a good job of persuading her that the benefits of a boarding school education far outweighed the negatives.

I would always be around other pupils, who would be in the same position as me, and having others in the same boat is beneficial. If I was struggling with a particular subject, then I would easily be able to stay after a lesson and go over the material with my teacher without worrying about how I would get home if I stayed late. For my dad, these were valid reasons for enrolling me in a boarding school. A good education was an investment for life, and my parents – particularly Dad – wanted all of their children to make the most of their education.

Mum looked anxiously at the three of us, as if for assurance from one or all of us that her child was going to be okay in these new surroundings.

"Good afternoon, madam, how are you?" Bobby asked politely.

"I am fine, thank you."

"I'm Bobby, the head prefect, and I will be looking after Brian while he studies here."

My mum looked noticeably less anxious when she heard that someone had been appointed to watch over me.

"Thank you so much, Bobby, please take good care of him. Brian is still young, and it will be difficult for him to be away from home. Also, do you go to church?"

"I do: although it isn't compulsory most of the pupils here attend church on Sundays. On a Wednesday we also have Bible studies in the dormitories, with general knowledge quizzes on Tuesdays and Thursdays after classes and meals."

I don't know if my mum took much notice of the latter part of Bobby's statement; she had her concerns about me often being around a large group of children my own age in my spare time, and that they may not continue showing respect to God without adult supervision. Mum smiled at me, pleased in the knowledge that my room mates were the kind of people who voluntarily attended church and tried to understand the Bible. I was unable to smile back.

Mum knew that I was unhappy at the prospect of leaving home; I hardly knew anyone, I was unsure what my daily routine would be and there would be nowhere private where I could go if I wanted to be alone. I even began to worry that the surroundings might have a negative impact on my school work; concentrating would be difficult when I would be surrounded by so many people, and it would be strange asking my teachers for help in the evenings when I always went to my dad.

I was concerned about meeting new people. Even though I had moved schools several times already, it was still daunting to me. I had always been quite reserved; I enjoy the company of other people, but I had always been much more comfortable being alone than with other children of my age. Nonetheless, I didn't want to attend a school and have no friends.

I only managed one look at my parents before they got into the car; Mum was crying silently, and even Dad's eyes were red. I knew they were both going to miss me, but I also knew I had to stay here and make them proud. I looked at the floor until the sound of the car faded away. I felt a hand on my shoulder and I looked up to see Bobby giving me an encouraging smile. I knew he was trying to comfort me, but it had the opposite effect; I didn't know him, so it just made me feel even more alone. I walked away and Bobby followed slowly behind. He led me to my dormitory bed where there were around forty other pupils.

Chapter Twelve

What Lies Ahead

My first day in boarding school was far from exciting. I had no friends with whom I could socialise, so the day passed by slowly. We were shown around the school and it looked as if it hadn't been redecorated for years. Walking from dormitory to dormitory to be introduced to other pupils made me feel even more alone; they were all in the same position as me but they seemed excited and interested. I didn't feel the same way as they did.

Bobby came to find me in the evening when lessons had finished; he told me that he had come to see if I was okay after my first day. Even though he was kind and attentive, he was still a stranger to me so I made my excuses, "I'm feeling really tired after my first day, do you mind if I go to lie down?"

"Of course not. Oh… before you go, do you have an alarm clock?"

"No, should I have one?"

I was confused by this. I didn't remember an alarm clock being on the list of things to bring to the new school.

"It's not an essential item. Some pupils just prefer to have their own. It's not a problem that you don't have one; the dormitory alarm will sound at 6am. After that the prefect will ring a bell, signalling that all the pupils must begin getting ready."

I wasn't accustomed to waking up at this time; my parents woke me at 7.30am and that was often a struggle. Even though I felt extremely irritated by this, I didn't have the energy to protest; I knew that if I spoke another word, I was likely to burst into tears. I simply nodded my assent to Bobby, and walked to my bed.

I noticed that more and more pupils were beginning to arrive in the dormitory; it was usually the case that the older pupils didn't begin lessons until the day after the new pupils had arrived, so that they would have some time to adjust to the school when it was slightly quieter. I had thought my dormitory being so close to the classroom was an advantage but it now seemed like a distinct disadvantage when I was trying to sleep. We were right next to the main hall; I could clearly hear the sound of suitcases being dragged along the floor and families saying their goodbyes. Even though I had left Bobby for the quiet seclusion of my bed, I didn't think I'd be able to get much sleep now.

Lessons in the new academic setting were very challenging and the teachers had strict rules. All pupils had to arrive on time. Arriving late resulted in punishments. The only language spoken in the school was English. Although it was a multi-cultural environment with pupils coming from different backgrounds and with different languages, we weren't allowed to bring up any cultural differences or to speak our native languages. Speaking any language other than English resulted in punishments which mostly involved being whipped by the teacher if it occurred in the classroom or, if it was outside the classroom, the older pupils had the authority to punish the younger pupils as they saw fit.

Although my English was much improved, it still wasn't perfect. It was a combination of broken Pidgin English and what in those days we called simple clear English. I still spoke the native Isoko language more fluently than English. I also spoke other local dialects such as Ibo, Urhobo and other languages.

I mostly kept quiet to avoid being punished, as I wasn't totally confident and comfortable with my English but this didn't stop the older pupils from bullying me and other younger pupils. Whenever the older pupils had the chance, they would take advantage: ordering us to go to the shops to buy items for them, without giving us enough money. If we questioned them, they felt insulted and we got extensive punishments. If we complained, the punishments were increased. For these reasons, I couldn't even give a clue to Bobby about what was happening.

Eventually, one day, I was tasked by an older pupil to insult my parents for no apparent reason. I refused. He was so annoyed with me for disobeying him that he called on some of his classmates to pick on me. I stood my ground. They punched me and slapped me but I still refused to abuse my parents. Fortunately, another older pupil who was older than the bullies came to the rescue and explained to Bobby what had happened. Bobby traced the bullies and gave them a good whipping. I was hurt but remained tough. Soon after, I heard that being part of the Nigerian Army Cadets in the school would deter any older pupil from bullying me and or others who were younger. I enrolled to join. The process was really tough but I went through it successfully. Just before I was to have my uniform, which I would carry with me when not in my school uniform to give me the authority to challenge any possible bully, I was told that half term was coming. I was disappointed. I wanted the authority given to me by the Nigerian Army Cadet to take on my bullies, but felt that I would have to wait until the next term to do so.

One night, I went to bed with the thoughts of progressing in the army. While I was asleep, I had a dream: I had been targeted by an individual who touched me. Immediately after the touch, I couldn't hear anything. I was alarmed and dashed to my brother Eugene. He asked what had happened. I murmured to him and he screamed for help from our relatives nearby. Everyone took chase to catch the individual, who had run into a crowd of carnival dancers and so it wasn't possible to get hold of him. This shocked and scared me and then I woke up. It was still very dark, possibly the middle of the night. I looked at the other pupils around me but they were all still fast asleep. I couldn't get back to sleep again. I was concerned about what had happened and wondered if it was real or just a bad dream. As everyone else was still asleep, I couldn't test my hearing, to know if it was just a dream or not. I waited for some sounds. Then came some footsteps; a pupil was going to the toilet. I heard those footsteps and felt the thud of them, which reassured me that I had just had a terrible dream and I tried to sleep again, but I couldn't. The wake-up bell sounded. Pupils began to rush for a shower. I tried to do the same but having not slept since that dream, I didn't have the energy to dash for the shower. I began to feel that I wasn't well as I had a migraine. My body temperature was very high and all my muscles were aching. My mate Ugo came to ask why I wasn't getting up for breakfast and for lessons. I told him that I wasn't well and he said he would tell the head prefect, Bobby, and the teacher that I was poorly. I thanked Ugo and went back to sleep.

It was several weeks later that I became conscious enough to realise that I was very ill, that I had been rushed to hospital and had been there for some weeks. I was even moved from one hospital to another but was unaware that that had happened. I was so very weak that I forgot about the dream. Strangely, I heard no sounds. I couldn't communicate with anyone and the doctors said it was because I wasn't well. I saw children crying, but I thought, because it was at the hospital children were allowed to cry without making any noise. I went back to sleep again. When I woke up, my parents were around me with my relatives. I wanted to go to the toilet, got out of the bed and fell down. My legs couldn't balance properly. I received support to walk to the toilet and back to the bed. The doctor told my Dad that I had suffered from meningitis, which had affected my brain and therefore my capability to hear, balance and walk. Dad said that I had been treated at the previous hospital for malaria. The present doctor said that it was not malaria but meningitis and because the treatment I had been given was wrong and too late, there might have been some damage to my sensory capability. I saw Mum crying. Dad spoke to me. I looked at him and was able to respond. Unknown to me at that time, I was naturally lip-reading my dad. Dad thought something wasn't right. Why didn't I respond when something was dropped behind my back? Dad decided to ask me the same question while standing behind me. I didn't hear him, so I did not reply. It was then that Dad and the doctor concluded that I had lost my hearing. Mum was told about this. She cried and cried and held me tightly to her, screaming, "Why, why, why?"

I wasn't sure what was happening and thought the illness was temporary and that I would be fully cured in time to come.

I was about twelve years old when I was discharged from the hospital and taken home. I could no longer communicate with my siblings - I couldn't hear what they were saying. I couldn't hear the telephone ringing and I couldn't hear the radio. I tried to listen to other sounds, so, I deliberately dropped some metal objects but I couldn't hear them. I was devastated. Mum would come to me to ask me questions. I couldn't understand her. My mother cried and cried as she couldn't bear it.

Dad didn't give up. He continued to find other opportunities for me. Eventually, he decided that, as I was born in London it would be worth sending me there for medical treatment. Dad had heard of Great Ormond Street Children's Hospital. He arranged as fast as he could, within a few weeks, to send me to London.

It was three o'clock in the morning when my dad came in to wake me for the journey to London but unbeknown to him, I hadn't slept at all. Throughout the night unanswered questions had been constantly on my mind. How cold will it be in London? What food do they eat? Can they find a way for me to hear again? I got up and sat on the edge of the bed, to show my dad that I wasn't asleep but I just didn't want to move. I couldn't find the motivation to begin the long journey to England. I couldn't bear the thought of being so far away from my family again and the life that I knew, however if I wanted to get better this was my only chance.

The lights were turned down as the plane engine started; it had only gone a few metres forwards when our heads were suddenly forced back against the seats as the plane began to ascend. I shut my eyes and pretended to sleep, while my mind drifted to the past.

"Goodbye Mum, bye bye Mummy," I called to her.

I remembered the tears in my mum's eyes as she held me for the last time. I can still remember saying goodbye to my brothers and sisters, and they envied me for the journey I was about to undertake to England. What they didn't know was that I would have swapped the entire experience, just to stay at home with my family and let somebody else take my place in England with the tragedy that I have just suffered.

Seeing my mum crying broke my resolve. I cried as the plane took off and was comforted by Dad. In no time, I fell asleep. Dad woke me up for meals now and then, but I would fall back into my quiet world. I'd ask myself countless times, 'Why me, why me…?'

I would then try to listen to any sound around. I saw the air hostess talking to the passengers in front of us but I couldn't hear what she was saying. I clenched my teeth so tightly with frustration, 'Why me, why me...?'

I cried silently in this quiet world, thinking about what the future would be like for me. I wondered if I would be cured and how excited I would be once I was back to 'normal'. I fell back into deep thoughts. Thinking back about all the music, the telephone conversations, the laughing and dancing I had enjoyed through my life. The sound of birds singing, the various accents of those from different tribes, the musical car horns, the screams of those in arguments and fights and the sounds of my family's voices. Mum's voice was always gentle and comforting. Dad's was strong but encouraging. Brothers' and sisters' voices were cheeky, but soft. Would I ever be able to hear these again? How would I cope at school? Would I even be able to return to the school to continue with my education? I was just beginning to settle down there. I enjoyed the lessons, sports such as boxing, football, and track and field athletics and the other tough challenges I faced in the cadet training sessions. I was beginning to find my identity as a young man; planning ahead for a successful career. I had enjoyed Interhouse Debates between the various dormitories at Government College, Ughelli such as: 'Chicken or Egg: Which Came First?' We had to give evidence to support our case. I was particularly good at this, which made me think of a career within the legal profession. I could become a lawyer and put forward good arguments and evidence to support my clients' cases. If I couldn't make it in the legal profession, I could become a teacher, a sportsman or simply a successful businessman. I didn't want to be lazy, living off my parents and doing nothing at home.

In the few months at Government College, I had got to know a few people who I could call friends; people I trusted and relied on for personal and emotional support but now what lay ahead in my future?

I tried to remain silent with my cries, but suddenly I could no longer hold them, started shaking and broke out crying. Dad looked at me, gave me a cuddle and stroked my hair. He took the tissue in front of him and used it to wipe the tears from my cheeks and encouraged me to blow my nose. For a while I remained silent, but the tears continued flowing down my cheeks through the blanket that wrapped around me in the cold dark plane. I felt them running down my neck, soaking my shirt and the vest underneath. I continued to wonder about all those sounds I was missing and might miss for the rest of my life, or would this loss of hearing be temporary? I looked up at the ceiling of the plane; most of the lights were off and the little tiny bulbs shining randomly around the plane like bright little stars couldn't reveal the answers that I was seeking. I imagined that as I could not hear anything, the plane was in complete silence, but I wondered how a plane with both adults and little children could fall completely silent for the duration of the journey. An air hostess marched past, but I could not hear her footsteps. Maybe there are no sounds in aeroplanes? While I was deep in thought, Dad suddenly asked me a question, as though he could hear my inner concerns. I just nodded but I couldn't hear what he had asked. I looked at Dad's face to check if I had answered him correctly with the nod, but the look on his face showed me that I hadn't, and he felt as bad as me that I could no longer hear him. I could feel that Dad was also hurting inside, sharing my agonies. Dad had done so much for me since my birth and having the solutions for my hearing loss was a bigger challenge than Dad could have prepared for. I continued to think of my hearing life, my current situation and what lay ahead, crying silently until I fell asleep again in the dampened blanket.

It was when the aeroplane touched down that I woke up and again began to feel emotional. Landing in a strange country far, far away from home; without access to sound, my brothers, sisters, friends and especially to my mummy, tore me to pieces. My heart was fully broken. Tears rolled down my cheeks as I thought back to **when mother cried.**

****

Endnotes

Biafran War 6th July 1967 to 15th January 1970

Nigeria gained independence from Britain in 1960, but remained in the Commonwealth. The conflict resulted from political, economic, ethnic, cultural and religious tensions, which preceded Britain's formal decolonization of Nigeria from 1960 to 1963. Basically, there were three ethnic groups in the Country: the Yoruba in the SW, who were mainly Christian, the Igbo in the SE, which is where there are huge oil deposits, and the Hausa and Fulani in the North who were predominantly Muslim. A conservative estimate is that over one million people died in the Civil War (Wikipedia)

Engineer (Chief) Wilson Diejeta Kokoruwe JP

After acquiring all his degrees in the United Kingdom, Brian's father had just one burning desire, which was to bring home his wealth of knowledge to benefit the larger Nigerian society. On his return to Nigeria in 1972, he was appointed to Auchi Polytechnic as a Lecturer in the Engineering Faculty. Before his appointment, there were only volunteer service graduates from overseas (VSO) working as lecturers with Nigerian Technical instructors. He was the head of the Electrical/Electronics Engineering Department, as well as Head of the

School of Engineering; being the first indigenous graduate posted to the Polytechnic. He functioned in this dual capacity until 1975, before joining the Petroleum Training Institute as a Lecturer. He rose through the ranks to Chief Lecturer and later Deputy Director (of Training), retiring in 1999.

In recognition of his towering contributions to the development of his community and to humanity, Brian's father was bestowed with the Chieftaincy titles of Elo of the Owhe and the Okugbe of Orugun Kingdoms. He was also sworn as a Justice of Peace (JP) by the Chief Judge of Delta State Government in 1997. He is a fellow of Delta State Polytechnic, Ozoro.

Chief Wilson Diejeta Kokoruwe is a devout Anglican Christian. He was baptised and confirmed in 1957 at All Saints Anglican Church, Yuba. He has remained firmly in the faith, even through his stay abroad. He is married to two wives and blessed with fourteen children, many grandchildren, a great grandchild and other relatives. All of his fourteen children are graduates, doing well in different endeavours.

As a retiree, a great grandfather and an accomplished scholar, he reads books in his leisure time. He has also retired to farming as a means of whiling away the time.

Meningitis

Brian contracted meningitis when he was about twelve years of age and living in Nigeria. Outbreaks of bacterial meningitis occur between December and June each year in a swathe of sub-Saharan Africa (see below), which has been plagued by large epidemics of meningococcal meningitis for over a century, leading it to be labelled the Meningitis Belt.

Sub Saharan Meningitis Belt

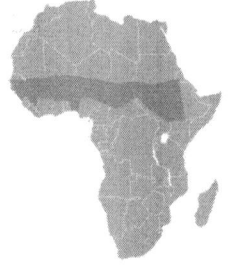

The largest epidemic ever recorded in history swept across the entire region in 1996-1997, resulting in 250,000 cases and causing 25,000 deaths.

Meningitis can be life threatening because of the inflammation's proximity to the brain and spinal cord, therefore the condition is classified as a medical emergency. Socio-economic and demographic factors as well as geographical mobility, such as that experienced in

Nigeria, with movement of large numbers of people during the Civil War, are causative factors.

In children there are several potential disabilities which may result from damage to the nervous system including sensori-neural loss, epilepsy, learning and behavioural difficulties as well as decreased intelligence. These occur in about 15% of survivors.

****

It will be apparent to the reader, that Brian's father had high aspirations for his son, who had himself gained his degree in Britain and worked for BP in his country of birth. The young Brian Kokoruwe was in due course dispatched to England to receive medical attention for his illness and to further his education. The background to this event so unfolds...